Praise for Demystifying College Admission

"This is a must-read for guidance counselors, parents, and students who want the edge! Regardless of your background or financial situation, you can go to college. Brian will show you how. *Demystifying College Admission: Learn Key Strategies and Develop the Right Mindset to Get into the College of Your Choice* will help alleviate the fear and stress of getting into college through innovative solutions and time-tested strategies."

-**Havilah Malone, author of** *You Came to Win! 31 Day Guide to Confidently Unleash Your Gifts & Create a Life of Massive Success*

"In today's competitive environment, *Demystifying College Admission: Learn Key Strategies and Develop the Right Mindset to Get into the College of Your Choice* is THE go-to guide for students of all ages. By giving you a game plan for success, Brian Keith South puts you in the win column! It's your choice. Make it the right one."

-**Glen E. Gibbs, author of** *Remodel Your Mindset: Be More Do More Have More*

"A masterful debut into a powerful story that demystifies college admission! It's impossible to read this book without thinking differently about the choices we can make for college admission."

-**Colleen Fedigan-Walski, author of** *Growing into Greatness.*

It's all here: anything one needs to know for preparation in the college admission process, from mindset to task planning. The way that Brian uses the gems of sage business leaders—like Zig Ziglar and Napoleon Hill—is fun. He is able to share some real-life stories to help families embrace the journey of college admissions. This book is complete.

-**Lee Rosenblum, Financial Advisor Representative**

"If you are NOT interested in playing Russian roulette with your money, time, and future, read *Demystifying College Admission: Learn Key Strategies and Develop the Right Mindset to Get into the College of Your Choice!* Brian South will place you on the right road. He will help you devise a plan of action. His get ready, aim, and focus advice is relevant to all aspiring collegians, regardless of their economic or social background.

-Dr. Virginia LeBlanc, author of *Love the Skin YOU'RE in: How to Conquer Life through Divergent Thinking*

"Wow! That was my reaction when I first read the testimonial of one of Brian South's students who got into the college of his choice using the methods outlined in the book. It read like a novel, entertaining, engaging, and very candid. Then I noticed that the chapters are full of content and current statistics that are bound to help parents prepare their child for higher education. Every important facet of the process is explained chapter by chapter. It is like an encyclopedia that reads like a novel. 5 stars to Brian South. He has a valuable resource that has taken a dry topic and made it into an art form."

-Randy Taylor, Certified Marketing Coach

"With depth, character, and ingenuity, Brian captures the immediate attention of the reader from the get-go! This book provides an insightful, straightforward, step-by-step approach to college admission. Not only does this book give insightful and a natural step-by-step approach to college admission, but it also reaches into the depths of your soul, inspiring you to push yourself to new limits. This book is for all students of life wishing to master a more natural way to live."

-Kathy Tuccaro, author of *Dream Big!*

Demystifying
College Admission

Demystifying College Admission

Learn Key Strategies and Develop the Right Mindset to Get into the College of Your Choice!

by Brian Keith South

CINNAMON TREE PRESS

A Carnelian Moon Publishing Inc., Imprint

Published by Cinnamon Tree Press, an
Imprint of Carnelian Moon Publishing

www.carnelianmoonpublishing.com

Copyright © 2020 Brian Keith South

All Rights Reserved. No part of this book may be reproduced, distributed, or transmitted in any form or by any means, electronic or mechanical, including photocopying and recording, or by any information storage and retrieval system, without express permission in writing from the publisher. The only exception is by a reviewer, who may quite short excerpts in a review.

Cover design by Jennifer Insignares
Interior design by Simon Brimble

Hardback ISBN: 978-1-7354333-1-8
Paperback ISBN: 978-1-7354333-2-5
eBook ISNB: 978-1-7354333-0-1

Library of Congress Control Number: 2020913992

Printed in the United States of America

CONTENTS

ACKNOWLEDGMENTS	1
FOREWORD	7
PREFACE	13
CHAPTER 1	**17**
Desire is the Firepower of College Admission	17
What is a Mission Statement?	20
Vision Statement	22
CHAPTER 2	**27**
Organized Planning: The Roadmap for College Admission	27
Keys to Developing an Organized Effective College Admissions Plan	30
Prioritizing Actions	32
Enslaved to Desperation	33
The Push to Nowhere	35
Categories of Daily Activities	36
CHAPTER 3	**43**
Making the Decision Toward College Admission	43
My Personal Story of College Decision	44
What Will You Become?	45
The Importance of Setting Goals	47
S.M.A.R.T. GOALS	47
A Match Made in Heaven	51
CHAPTER 4	**55**
Faith–The Mighty Thought Force of College Admission	55
Alchemy of Faith	55

Winter of Opportunity	56
The Antidote for the Protective Mind	58
Suspend, Transcend and Ascend	58
No Such Thinking as Random Misfortune	59
Faith Empowers the Mind	60
Avoid the Dark Zone	61
CHAPTER 5	**63**
The Practicality of Passion in Choosing a Major	63
Apply the Lean Startup Principle	68
A Whole New Mind Shift	72
CHAPTER 6	**75**
Taking the Test Drive	75
CHAPTER 7	**85**
Virtuoso Interviews for College Admissions	85
Before the Interview	86
Prepare to Answer the Following Questions:	86
After the Interview	92
CHAPTER 8	**95**
The Importance of Obtaining Great Letters of Recommendation	95
Who is a Good Candidate for a Letter of Recommendation?	96
When Should I Ask for a Letter of Recommendation?	96
What Information Should I Supply My Recommenders?	97
How to Make a Request	98
The Logistics of the Recommendation	99
How Should You Ask for a Letter of Recommendation from Your School Counselor?	99
Are My Letters Confidential?	100

Your Rights Under FERPA	101
Following Up with Recommendation Requests	101
CHAPTER 9	**103**
The Brave New World of College Application Basics	103
What Happens if You Miss a Deadline?	104
The Advantages and Disadvantages of Applying Early	106
Early Decision Musts	107
CHAPTER 10	**111**
Writing the Essay of Champions	111
Why the Essay is Important	113
Who Will Read Your Essay?	113
Typical Essay Questions:	114
The One-Paragraph Essay	118
Submit Academic Writing	118
Avoid These Practices	120
Grammar Considerations	121
Transitions	122
Write in the Active Voice	122
Show, Don't Tell	122
Steps to Writing the Essay	122
CHAPTER 11	**125**
The Rudiments of Financial Aid	125
The Fundamentals of Financial Aid	127
Family Outing at the Financial Aid Office	127
Need-Based Aid Versus Merit-Based Aid	128
Merit-Based Aid	128
What are Need-Based Aid Scholarships?	129

Determining Student Financial Needs — 129
  Pell Grant — 130
  FAFSA (Free Application for Federal Student Aid) — 130
  Where to obtain more knowledge about Financial Aid — 130

CHAPTER 12 — 133
  Finding the Money so That Money Finds You the College of Your Choice — 133
  Important Steps to Finding a Scholarship — 135
  Making the Grade — 135
    Write an Amazing Essay — 135
    How to Write an Engaging Essay — 136
  Six Great Sites to Look for Scholarships — 138

CHAPTER 13 — 141
  The Right Major at the Right College at the Right Time — 141

CHAPTER 14 — 155
  College Admissions on the House — 155
    When Should I Apply for Student Housing? — 156
  Amenities — 161
    On-Campus Apartments — 162
    Off-Campus Housing — 162
  The Cost of Student Housing to Tuition — 165
    How Do the Needy Find Resources for College Housing? — 166
    How Do Students Choose the Right Housing? — 167

CHAPTER 15 — 169
  Ready, Aim, Focus! — 169

CHAPTER 16 — 181
  Arresting the Misconceptions of the Incarcerated — 181

CHAPTER 17	195
Demystifying College Admission for Adults	195
Why Go to College?	196
Concerns Facing Adult Learners	199
Strategies for Adult Learners	204
Before You Hang Your Hat	205
Enroll Part-Time During Your First Year	206
Screen Potential Instructors	207
CHAPTER 18	213
Special Needs and College Admission	213
What Are Special Needs Students?	213
Medical Issues	215
ADHD Symptoms	215
Preparing Special Needs Students for College	217
Applying Concerns for Special needs	217
ADHD and College Admission	218
Medication and ADHD	219
Why You Must Receive Accommodations	221
Know Your Legal Rights as a Special Needs College Student	222
CHAPTER 19	225
Fostering College Admissions Against the Wind	225
Against the Odds	225
Misconceptions about Foster Students	227
An Oasis Where Foster Children Thrive	229
Essential Steps for Foster Students Applying to College	231
How Can Instructors Help?	234
What Reaources Are Available for foster Students?	239

Foster Care to Success: America's College Fund for Foster Youth ... 240

CHAPTER 20 ... 249
Artificial Intelligence: The College of Tomorrow—Today ... 249
What Is Artificial Intelligence? ... 250
How Will Artificial Intelligence Affect College Application? ... 250
How will AI impact the classroom? ... 251
How Can AI Help with College Admission? ... 253
AI and the Humanities? ... 255
How can College Students Prepare for the AI Future Today? ... 257
Humans Rule ... 259

CHAPTER 21 ... 263
E-Learning and College Admission ... 263
What Is Distant Learning? ... 264

FINAL WORD ... 269
WORKS CITED ... 271
TESTIMONIAL STORIES FROM STUDENTS AND PARTNERS ... 277
INDEX ... 286
AUTHOR TESTIMONIALS ... 291
ABOUT THE PUBLISHERS ... 295

ACKNOWLEDGMENTS

Crafting this college admissions book for the past two years has taught me that even a solo, lifetime accomplishment such as writing a book is a collaborative effort. I could never have completed *Demystifying College Admission* without the support, encouragement, and advice I received from many. I want to thank Hari Shetty, my supervisor, colleague, and friend. He has selflessly promoted me. Hari has provided me with amazing students whom I have had the pleasure of mentoring for more than nine years at EZ Tutoring. He has also introduced me to Jothi Periasami, Chief Data Scientist at Experfy, a premier artificial intelligence teacher at MIT. Jothi's vision is to bring an enterprise view to academic concepts and demonstrate practical business problem-solving techniques through proven industry use cases. He selflessly worked with me in completing a chapter on college admissions and artificial intelligence. I am fortunate for the support, mentorship, and endorsement I received from Anna Miller-Tiedeman, President of the New Careering Institute. She taught me that life is our career; there are no mistakes, just left turns instead of the right ones. She inspired me to embrace legendary thought leaders like Stephen Covey, Napoleon Hill, Jim Rohn, and several others mentioned in this book. I don't know what I would do without Mel Vesley, the extreme makeover man. He helped me with my public image and introduced me to Joy Porter, an amazing woman with a magic eye who took stunning photos of me.

Thanks to Elias Melas and Aaron Hammock for promoting me on their radio show, "The Morning Rooster." I appreciate Steve Robello, who took the time to interview with me and provide me with three amazing clients from Hawaii. Deborah Kaplan from Home Tutoring Plus deserves special recognition. She recruited me for my first tutoring position. She introduced me to my life-changing profession of mentoring the world's future leaders and achievers. I appreciate Randy Taylor, sales trainer, actor, published since 1998, and quoted in *Forbes*. He is the reason why I learned many things about multi-media and networking. I want to shout praise and thanks to Chris Voght. I made many connections through his fantastic program called Attraction Marketing Builds Relationships. In particular, he introduced me to Athina Salazar (Chief Possibility Officer) and Denver Vo (Certified Hypnotherapist). They are two incredible people who inspire and support anyone seeking to develop a positive money mindset and self-esteem. Chris also introduced me to Berny Dohrmann, who founded CEO Space International

25 years ago. Berny taught me to emphasize in my marketing that it will "cost clients nothing to explore, just explore and that they will never leave, once they believe." I owe thanks to Alan Fahden, CEO Innovation on Demand, author corporate trainer who selflessly helps everyone despite his prominent standing as a consultant to Fortune 500 companies. He taught me to dare to embrace my uniqueness in motivating students to grow and prosper. I want to thank Dr. Malaika Singleton, CEO of Saint Nia, who appointed me as a board member. Malaika introduced me to Jody Lowen. Jody is the founder and executive director of the Prison University Project at San Quentin. She shares my belief that everyone, regardless of background, deserves an education. I acknowledge Ed Smelich and Lee Rosenblum from World Financial Group. They provide a wealth of information to help families save their wealth in college planning. Claire Van Niekerken has also helped me with getting my life insurance license and promoted me. I appreciate Hermie Backus, who gave priceless information about how families can save on the ticket price of college and Jodi Smaltz for introducing me to Hermie. Also, I am grateful to John C. Shin, Founder, CEO, and President of Axianta. He inspired me to embrace Napoleon Hill's concepts, mentioned throughout this book.

Additionally, Clarizcel Roxas Senior Marketing Director of Axianta and Dennis Saicoci encouraged me to incorporate the concepts of Napoleon Hill in my work. Through regular meetings in a Think and Grow Rich networking, I have been learning and putting abundance into action. I am thankful for Cami Ferry (Theater Queen) and Jim Chong (Work Star), who invited me to advertise my book on their radio show, "The Rush Hour of Success." I am grateful for the inspiration, collaboration, and motivation I received at the Get Motivated Seminar. At this life-changing convention, I met Gerry Roberts, who hosted *Publish a Book and Grow Rich*, the birthplace of this book. I appreciate Andrea Elena Halikia. She held me accountable in the Kick in the Butt publishing program.

I have met several dear friends and fellow authors because of Andrea. I am thankful for Colleen Fedigan-Walski, founder and CEO of the Scott Foundation. She has been a wonderful friend, support, a champion of foster youth, and just a fantastic person in every way. Dr. Virginia LeBlanc has been very supportive and collaborative as a fellow author, and advocate for education. I can't thank her enough for supporting me in writing this book. Havilah Malone, the publicity magnet, has been amazing. She has helped my vision of college admission and introduced me to Justin Bayer, CEO and Founder of Welcome to College.

I thank Kathy Tuccaro for her friendship, support, feedback, and inspiration to live with purpose, passion, and power. She has encouraged me to Dream Big! Glen Gibbs has been an inspiration and incredible support in finding content for this book. I want to thank my Aunt Carol, who encouraged me to become an author and speaker. I appreciate my Aunt Dalia's undying support and belief in me. I am grateful to all the students I have worked with over the years. They have been a constant source of joy, inspiration, and growth. I thank River Easter, who advised, supported, and re-wired me for success! Also, the Millionaire Mindset has been amazing. It has taught me to think with abundance, identify my money blueprint, and network like a racehorse! Paul Bozzo, from SCORE, provided many invaluable tips on branding, marketing, and promoting my work.

I want to shout out praise to Colette Smithers, who did a stunning job of writing my biography. I am thankful for the Art of Living and the teachings of Sri Sri Ravi Shankar. Nikki Myres, my fiancée, has loved me, supported me, and has stuck with me in the best and worst of times during the writing of this book. I would also like to thank Vladimir Francois, for his wisdom and editing elegance.

I thank Darlene Julyanto for her amazing editing and feedback about making my writing more down-to-earth.

Words alone could never express my gratitude for everyone at Carnelian Moon Publishing for their tireless support, generosity, and belief in my book. In particular, I thank Debbie Belnavis-Brimble for her ingenious insights, organization, planning, strategies, and resources to reach a wider readership audience. I appreciate Simon Brimble's amazing editing and layout design. I thank Judith Richardson Schroeder for her support and stunning editing during the final draft. I appreciate Jennifer Insignare's incredible, beautifully design book cover.

Thank you, everyone!

FOREWORD

School! As you read that word, you most likely uttered it in such a way that it included a sigh or a grunt. Exams, flat-out annoying classmates, often unqualified teachers…you know the story. Growing up in a Desi-American family, where my elders often stressed the importance of education, I felt pressured to perform at an optimum level. Simply attaining 90% on an assignment or exam was not enough. "Oh, an A-? Why couldn't you get 100%? Why did you not study enough?" was the standard response I would get from my kin if I was not perfect. As a result, I lost the motivation to excel in academics. Why should I

RAM SHARMA
In front of the podium at the White House for his first internship in Washington D.C. through the Mellenial Action Project. He became a Wayne Morse Scholar and author. Now he is Phi Betta Cappa graduate of the University of Oregon in 2020. He is applying to law school.

continue to work my butt off when it was never enough? Subjects such as math, science, and history became like dark clouds on a cold night in December to me: dreadful!

To add insult to the injury, my grades fell off dramatically, especially in the areas I had always *deemed* evil: English, writing, and grammar. To me, those areas of academia seemed like tools in a mechanic shop. No life, just numerous rules and regulations; constant "thou shalts and thou shalt nots" were part of my daily routine. By the time I entered seventh grade, I was a 2.5 GPA student – trust me, I still have those report cards that I look back at every time to reminisce on my struggles. My family was disappointed, perplexed, and outraged by my performance. They decided that it was time to seek out a tutor that would get me back on track… back onto the path of *success*. It was the start of seventh grade. I was ready for a school year of going with the flow, having fun, and ignoring my academic responsibilities. I came back from school one day and entered my house excited to go play Xbox! I had just gotten NBA 2K9 with my favorite player of all time on the cover, Kevin Garnett. The *last* thing I wanted to do was do my homework! Before I could start balling out with Garnett, my family came to me and informed me that I would be meeting with a tutor who would help me with English, writing, and grammar… the whole enchilada. In reaction, my face dropped. What's the point? Even if this tutor could help me, it still wouldn't be enough for my family or myself.

I waited in my room for this tutor, unaware that my life was going to change dramatically for the better. He came in, proceeded to sit down by me, and introduced himself.

"Hi Ram! My name is Brian South, and I am excited to work with you this school year."

"Me too," I sighed.

Our first couple of tutoring sessions were more meet and greets and getting to know each other as we embarked on this journey of success together. By our third session, we began to work on an essay that I had been given by my English teacher. We were required to write a fictional story ranging from 3-4 pages. Our teacher gave us so many guidelines on how she wanted it done. Thou shalt do this, thou shalt do that! Honestly, I was hoping Brian would do the essay for me.

We decided to do a story about a group of friends encountering danger and despair on what was supposed to be a day of happiness and excitement. We coined it: *Bonded Through Fear*. Brian began to explain to me that I could make writing into an art form despite the rules and regulations our teacher imposed upon us. He described to me the concept of *pizzazz*. Adding metaphors, similes, personification, high-level vocabulary words into my essay would make the process of writing *fun*. And that's what we did. We dramatized the story through all the writing techniques that he had drilled into my head. It was art. It was exciting. It was creative. And it was a 104% result…A++. For the first time, I did not feel shoved into a box of lifeless tools. I felt free in a new world of thrill, hype, and *pizzazz*. As a result of working with Brian, I discovered that writing isn't just a block of rules and regulations, but rather, it is a creative outlet that has opened up many doors of opportunity in my life. And yes, Brian wrote me a letter of recommendation for the scholarship and assisted me in my application essays.

I took Brian's *pizzazz* revelation and created my own revolution by applying it to all facets of life, including academia. In fact, the boy who once dreaded writing, grammar, and all areas of academics, has become an author. I have published a book titled, *Politics and the Global Impact of Inequality and Sexism*, which Brian helped edit even as I am now a junior in college at the University of Oregon (Go Ducks!). To this day, as I have become a 3.88 GPA student in college, Brian still assists me in my writing and has cultivated me into the student I am today. I have become the Vice-Chair of the Student Advisory Board at our Counseling Center and have been appointed into the student government as Accessibility Advocate. I became a Wayne Morse Scholar at the University of Oregon, a select group of 25 students who engage in praxis in questions regarding governance and democracy. And yes, Brian wrote me a letter of recommendation for the scholarship, a once in a lifetime professional and social experience in Washington D.C. that not many can attain. Before I departed for the trip, I met with Brian for his advice on personal and career goals I should set while interning in Washington D.C., *the greatest city in the world.* "Network, network, network," Brian repeated to me. He explained that being in a city where everyone is trying to become somebody, I need to be able to connect with professionals who can get me what I want while building relationships with them that will last a lifetime. I went to D.C. and returned with a professional network of 15+ individuals who range from White House Fellows to venture capitalists at the Carlyle Group. After speaking with these impressive D.C. insiders, I have come to realize what my career calling is and have discarded the idea of entering law school, which I had been debating on doing for quite some time. If Brian had never advised me to create a network and speak with as many people as possible, I would have never been able to realize that law is not my cup of tea and would have never acquired the amount of knowledge that I did while networking with D.C. professionals.

As a result of the personal growth and development I have experienced while under Brian South's mentorship, I highly recommend him to other students who are struggling with academics, who are seeking to grow in all facets of life besides academia, and who are searching for that *pizazz* in life that can propel them to unprecedented amounts of success as it has done for me. Brian has not only gifted me with his mentorship, but he has also given me his friendship. Through my highs and lows, Brian has stuck with me. He has celebrated my successes with me and has encouraged me to continue to push forward when I failed. *A mentor, motivator, writer extraordinaire pizzazz creator, friend*... Brian will no doubt, facilitate success and personal growth to whoever is blessed to be under his guidance.

Ram Sharma
Wayne Morse Scholar
University of Oregon

PREFACE

I wrote *Demystifying College Admission* because many students lack guidance in planning for college. Several foster youths, the incarcerated, older adults, and others feel they lack a voice in the college admission process. My book addresses these unique populations and provides guidance and resources for them to make college happen.

Also, I have discovered that the most significant challenges people encounter, aside from the high cost of college admission and the competition to get into good schools, is their mindset. They believe they are not smart enough or good enough to attend the college of their dream, so they engage in self-sabotaging behavior and give up. Therefore, I address the importance of purpose, organization, and the power of positive thinking as part of the college planning process and frame many of the chapters around legendary self-help authors, such as Napoleon Hill, Tony Robbins, Brian Tracy, Jim Rohn, and Stephen Covey. I suggest that you research any author or topic I mention to find out what concepts and techniques apply for you as a person and as a student. Perhaps you are an honor student. Or, you are in need of special accommodations or college funding.

What I learned in writing this book is that a central part of college admission is college funding. Many do not look at their finances when applying to schools. They are hoping that through a stroke of good luck, they will not only receive an admission letter, but they will also get full funding for room and board. While some students receive full scholarships that cover most of their college expenses, the majority take out expensive loans, drain their savings account. Some upper-middle-income parents told me that they did not believe their children could qualify for any scholarships or financial aid.

Moreover, I learned that many are underrepresented. Yet, there are plenty of resources online. The problem is that it is hard to find these resources without guidance and support. I included chapters that describe their dilemma and offer several resources to help them make college admission accessible.

As a result of the Coronavirus situation, our lives have been turned upside down. Within a month, students had to switch from in-person classes to online platforms overnight. The familiar landmarks of studying, preparing for college changed instantly. With accelerating technologies and the fallout of the pandemic there is uncertainty about the future of college. However, we can be certain about developing foundational coping skills that will serve us well in any time. Good health habits, self-awareness, focus, and determination are more important than ever. I include sources for traditional and nontraditional students. Read the chapters that apply to you and discard the rest. Feeling more confident, informed about applying to college is my objective in writing this book. Remember that success in college and beyond begins and ends in the mind.

CHAPTER 1

Desire is the Firepower of College Admission

Desire is the starting point of all achievement, not a hope, not a wish, but a keen pulsating desire which transcends everything.
Napoleon Hill.

Do you wake up every morning feeling overwhelmed about getting into college? Do you feel indecisive about where you want to attend and what you want to study? Do you think about career options after you graduate? Do you feel pressured by family and peers that you are futureless without college? Can you afford it? Is college the right choice for you?

The sobering statistics of the high cost of education would leave any applicant feeling concerned. According to a

Harvard website, the total 2018-2019 cost of attending Harvard for tuition, room, board, and fees is $67,580 (Harvard). So, you're looking at more than a quarter of a million dollars for your Harvard education, assuming that you're living on peanut butter sandwiches and Ramen noodles! According to the National Center for Education and Statistics, "In academic year 2017-18, the average net price of attendance (total cost minus grant and scholarship aid) for first-time, full-time undergraduate students attending 4-year institutions was $13,700 at public institutions, compared with $27,000 at private nonprofit institutions and $22,100 at private for-profit institutions (in constant 2018-19 dollars)" (Price). According to a U. S. News report, more than 100 colleges charge at least $50,000 for the current academic year (Kerr and Powell 2019). But even if money fell from the sky, you are still faced with the fiercely competitive nature of college admission.

Getting top-notch scores on placement exams is no guarantee that you will win the golden admission ticket. According to Wissner-Gross in *What Colleges Don't Tell You*, 107 out of the 300,000 students who achieved perfect scores on their SAT in 2005 did not guarantee placement.

In some of the most prestigious, Ivy League institutions, the requirements for admissions seem unattainable (Wissner-Gross, ch.1). Stanford has a 5% acceptance rate. Only 2,085 out of 44,073 applicants were admitted (Stanford Admission).

At Harvard, the average GPA is 4.04, and the acceptance rate is 5.2% (Harvard University). With such stringent requirements, how can a student even think of qualifying for college?

While no one can deny that college is expensive and outrageously competitive, there is light at the end of the college admission tunnel. There is hope. There are resources to help you get into the college of your choice. They all start with DESIRE. Be like fire. You cannot change the economy. You cannot wish away the competitive demands of admissions, but *you* can change.

If you become like fire and single-mindedly pursue your college dreams, you will be unstoppable. While college can be a vehicle to achieve a lucrative career and a better quality of life, college is about personal growth and development. Why wait until you spend thousands of dollars and countless hours of study? Why hope for the economy to improve and the admission requirements to soften? Achieve the best version of yourself right now—today—before you even apply. Jim Rohn says in *The Art of Exceptional Living*, "Don't wish it was easier; wish you were better. Don't wish for less problems; wish for more skills. Don't wish for less challenge; wish for more wisdom." (Givens, ch.3).

To fire your desire, you must define, refine, and confine your statement of purpose or mission statement. In *The Path*, bestselling author Laurie Beth Jones said that her uncle told her that an unidentified soldier would be shot on the spot if he could not state his mission. Imagine if we were all confronted with life and death decisions about college admission. Imagine submitting a clearly defined mission and vision statement. Imagine it all starting with you!

What is a Mission Statement?

According to Laurie Beth Jones in *The Path*, "a **mission statement** is a written-down statement that describes your reason for being. It is your key to finding your path. A mission statement will help you initiate, define, and refine all of your activities" (Jones, Intro). For college admission, a mission statement can help you decide your major and career path.

A good mission statement, according to Jones, contains the following qualities:
- It should not be longer than a single sentence.
- A 12-year old should easily understand it.
- One should recite it verbatim under threat of death (Beth-Jones).

In *The Path*, she provides a simple and effective strategy to write a mission statement within minutes, saving months, if not years of frustrating struggle, misplaced time of aimlessly and randomly applying for schools you don't like to impress people you do not know to find a prestigious job that does not exist.

While writing your mission statement is a simple, straightforward process, it may take a while for you to reflect on who you are, what you enjoy, how you like to express yourself and identifying your purpose. Find a quiet place that is cozy and comfortable. Grab a pen, a notebook, or your mobile device and feast on these food-for-thought questions:

- What makes you excited so that you want to leap out of bed early in the morning and go to sleep late at night?
- If you could teach something to a person or a group, what would it be? If you picked "justice" as the value that excites you, you might want to teach these three things:
  1. The world is fair and just.
  2. We must fight to preserve our liberty.
  3. There is justice all around us; it takes time, patience and skill to promote it.
- If you could convey three things in this world that enrage, sadden or intrigue you, what would they be?
- What subjects have you enjoyed studying in school?
- What areas of interest have you hidden?
- What makes you forget to eat?
- How are you going to save the world?
- If you knew that you were going to die one year from today, how would you want to be re- membered?
- If money was no object, and the opinions and judgment of others did not affect your choices, how

would you spend your time? What would you be doing every moment of the day for the rest of all your days?

After you answer all of these questions, the next step in completing your mission statement is to select three verbs corresponding to the desired activity. Laurie Beth Jones lists several verbs with a list of corresponding causes to form the main ingredients of a mission statement.

Here is an example of what a mission statement looks like:
My mission is to educate, empower, and inspire children to achieve academic excellence in public schools.

Vision Statement

A **vision statement** is the final result of your accomplishments. It is the vehicle that will drive you to your goals. As a college student, you will face many challenges that will test your resilience. Your vision will push you to the next level.

Here are the steps to writing your vision statement:

- **Write down your mission statement.** Do not trust your memory. Forgetfulness and humanity go hand-in-hand. Besides, writing your mission statement makes it real.
- **Write your vision in the present tense.** Our mind is only capable of processing the here and now. Expressing your desire to try and do something

tomorrow will not work.

- **Your vision should entail a wide range of activities and times.** List your weekday and weekend activities.
- **Your vision is visual, packed with sensory descriptions connected to reality.** We are physical beings who think with pictures and respond to sensory input.

Here is an example of a vision statement:

Four days per week, I am treating underprivileged children patients in a small brick office in the Lower East Side of Manhattan. I take their vitals, tell them stories, and educate their parents on how to keep them healthy. Once a month, I deliver speeches to community centers throughout the greater New York area. I inform the public about the high rate of infirm children in lower-income neighborhoods and how people in the community can band together to help them. As a result of my work, more than 40% of children in many underserved communities receive regular checkups and medicines for common illnesses. I have received generous donations through private funding and grants. People praise my work, and other health facilities want to model my approach to treating youth.

Based on the concepts of Napoleon Hill, there are six ways you can transmute your passion and desires into obtaining admission to the college of your choice:

1. Fix in your mind the exact kind of college you wish to attend. What is the name of this university? What field of study excites you? What is the physical appearance of your college? As you gain more knowledge, it is acceptable to change your focus. However, the clearer you are about where you want to attend, why you must attend, and what you will study, the more likely you are to get into the college of your dreams.

2. Determine exactly how you want to contribute to your university and society. There is no such thing as something for nothing. The admission committee has chosen you with the expectation that you will contribute significantly to its academic community and, in return, promise you with an education and the pedigree that will land you a career in your chosen field. Keep your mission and vision statement at hand. Your mission statement will help you determine how you will give back to your college and the world.

3. Establish a definite date when you expect to attend the college of your choice. The more specific you are, the more likely you are to make admissions a reality. The brain does not know the difference between reality and imagination. Once you establish in your mind a definite date that you are selected, admitted,

and enrolled in classes, the resources will suddenly appear to transmute your dreams into reality.
4. Create a definite plan to carry out your college admissions desire and begin at once. When you eventually target a specific school, you will need to create a schedule to meet deadlines for applications, submissions of transcripts, standardized tests, and financial aid. You need to start planning immediately because those deadlines approach sooner than you think. Start now. Start today.
5. Write a clear, concise statement of what career you will pursue once you graduate, when that career will begin, how much money you intend to make, and how much you plan to give back to society. Describe clearly the plan through which you intend to accumulate abundance.
6. Read your college admission plans daily, once upon rising in the morning and once before retiring at night. As you read your plan of action, see yourself already enrolled in the college of your dreams. Believe it is possible, and you will achieve it.

Whenever you are feeling pressured about getting into college because you are worried about the high costs and the stiff competition of college admission, remember that desire is the firepower that will make your college dreams come true. You will find the right people, resources, and support to make college happen, regardless of the inevitable challenges that you will face on your college journey. With a burning desire fueled with purpose and driven with a vision of why college admission is a must, you will be unstoppable. In the next chapter, you will learn the importance of organized planning in the college admission process.

CHAPTER 2

Organized Planning: The Roadmap for College Admission

First comes thought then comes organization of that thought into ideas and plans then comes the formation of those plans into reality.
Napoleon Hill.

Now that you've found the right college, and discovered your mission and vision for college admission, organized planning will ensure you're making the right choices and have the right mindset to secure your admission ticket. The first step to making sure that the college of your dreams becomes the college of reality is by forming definite, practical plans.

Align yourself with a mastermind group to support you. A mastermind group is a selection of peers or trusted individuals sharing a common interest to provide each other with advice and devise shared solutions to solve problems and achieve goals. Even though society encourages individuality, no one can succeed alone. When you combine sodium and chlorine, a metal with dangerous gas, you get something edible like table salt. It is much easier to write letter-perfect personal statements with several trusted eyes proofing your work. Preparing for interviews is a breeze if someone grills you with several questions that an employer, a professor, or admissions officer might ask. Write a list of all the people who could be part of your networking mastermind teams, such as parents, siblings, friends, teachers, employers, or even faculty and students at your selected school.

When you establish your mastermind group, decide how you will benefit everyone in your group. Remember the law of reciprocity: you must give something to receive something in return. Keep in mind the wise saying from John Lennon, "Life is what happens to you while you're making other plans." As you plan for college admission, you may encounter unexpected debt and personal setbacks. According to Murphy's law, "whatever can go wrong, will go wrong." Temporary defeat may seem discouraging and heartbreaking, but it can make you stronger, more resilient, and more effective as a student and as a well-developed human being. If your plans fail for any reason, develop new ones. Eventually, you will craft the master plan that lands you in college and prepares you to face unconquerable challenges and victories when you graduate. Before you put pen to paper, keep in mind the following attributes of a mastermind organized college planner:

Courage

Discovering the right major, the right career, and the right college to fulfill your dreams takes a lot of bravery. Even family and friends may attempt to discourage you from your college dreams. The world is full of doomsayers and naysayers. Follow your heart. Make a plan and take action on your terms.

Self-Control

As discussed later on, you must master yourself to master your success in college. Avoid procrastination, mindless pursuits that distract you from your college goals, and food that clouds the mind and infects your body. Surround yourself with supportive people who believe in you and support you.

Definiteness of Decision

Once you've identified the college of your choice, aim high, and concentrate all of your energy like a laser beam to achieving your admission ticket. Even if life distracts you, your determined efforts will pay off.

Definiteness of Plans

Napoleon Hill, Think and Grow Rich, "Plan your work and work your plan." Master all the details of your targeted college.

Keys to Developing an Organized Effective College Admissions Plan

You must spend time tracking your days. Setting your priorities, using a calendar, and working in a tidy workspace are essential steps in taking charge of your college admission.

1. *Organize Details for Admissions*

You can never be too busy to take all of the necessary steps to apply for the college of your choice.

2. *Do Not Worry About Competition from Others*

Remember that you are a unique individual. There is no one like you. No one can compete with your dreams, goals, self-discipline, and persistence.

3. *Aim High Above Mediocrity*

Though grades and standardized test scores are significant considerations in the college admissions process, they are not absolute measures of your self-worth. Grades can never measure your determination to strive for excellence in everything you do.

4. *Become Self-Made*

Keep in mind that college admission is a vehicle for academic achievement, vocational preparation, and personal development, but it is only one resource for achieving success. Do not fall into the complacency trap. Do not believe that breezing through your classes and receiving a degree will guarantee fame and fortune. You must develop a self-made mindset to make lifelong learning in and beyond college your goal. Read often, exercise, eat balanced meals, and take motivational seminars and business coaching.

5. Develop Self-Discipline

Rise early in the morning. Review your daily action plans for college admission. Exercise, eat well, and think positive thoughts. If you do not master yourself, you will be conquered by yourself, according to Napoleon Hill.

6. Embrace Proactiveness

Do not wait for the right time to prepare for the college of tomorrow—start now! The time will never be right! You need to act right now!

7. Do Not Expect Something for Nothing

The secret to success in college is not determined solely by grades, perfect test scores, diplomas, and prestigious titles. Even with the accolades of a college degree, you still need integrity and camaraderie with your community. Who you become is more important than your academic transcript. If you become the best version of yourself, everything around you will yield the best outcome for you.

8. Act Promptly and Decisively

According to Napoleon Hill, "successful people reach decisions promptly and change slowly." Once you decide on a college, commit to doing whatever it takes to receive admittance.

When you act quickly, you will be surprised to discover how quickly your college plans will fall into place.

Mindset Checklist

- Have I set a goal, organized it, written it down, and taken steps to achieve it?
- Have I been persistent in carrying out my college preparation plans to completion?
- Have I been proactive? Where did I allow the habit of procrastination to derail me?
- Did I keep an open mind about selecting the best college for myself?
- Have I budgeted my time and money with my educational goals?
- How much time have I spent in unprofitable activities that do not contribute to my college goals?

Prioritizing Actions

College admissions require lots of planning. You must list your activities on paper, prioritize them, and schedule them in a calendar. If you don't, you could feel easily overwhelmed and miss an important step. Burning the midnight oil may have worked in high school, but that strategy will not work in college. In *First Things First,* Dr. Stephen Covey, "encourages people to operate by **principles** as opposed to **values**." Principles are external, fixed, and governed by natural law. Values are internal and subjective beliefs and opinions (Covey, Intro). You might apply to a particular elite college because you value prestige and recognition. Are those truly your values? By operating on principles, you are performing according to natural, unchangeable laws. For instance, the seasons for planting and harvesting crops operate on principles. In March, when the weather warms, a farmer will prepare the soil for planting. In April or May, that farmer will plant seeds for corn, carrots, or cabbage. These plants may be ready to harvest within a month or perhaps several months later. Imagine what would happen if the farmer burned the midnight oil, as many students do, and planted the seeds in the winter, hoping they will sprout the very next day. What do you think would happen?

Imagine what life would be like if your college admission and vocational planning centered on principles? Imagine how you would feel if you organized your time effectively and planted seeds for success way before harvest time, such as the deadlines for applications, exams, and trips to prospective colleges. Do you believe you would feel less pressure, more fulfilled, and focused on goals most important to you?

Enslaved to Desperation

Do you often feel rushed to complete your assignments? Do you feel unprepared to perform well in an exam or write a stunning personal statement? Are you hurrying to blast out hundreds of applications to the most prestigious colleges on time, wondering and worrying if you will be selected? Are you feeling afraid that even if you are accepted, you are not sure if the Ivy League college you applied to is the right college for you?

According to Stephen Covey, "it is best to follow the compass instead of the clock." A composer, Glenn Holland (Richard Dreyfuss) in *Mr. Holland's Opus* desires to write a masterful music piece. Meanwhile, he takes a job as a music teacher at a high school in Oregon, hoping that he can support his family. At first, he hates his job because he thinks he is losing his golden chance to shine as a classical musician. He feels enslaved to the clock. Then he discovers that he loves teaching. He has found his purpose. He has found his compass.

As college applicants, use your internal compass while searching for the college of your dreams. Before you crack open an SAT study guide, frantically comb the internet for topnotch schools and commit needless hours in search of the perfect school that cannot even exist, ask yourself the following questions:

1. What is the one activity you can do right now that would provide you more clarity in choosing the best college or graduate program that is right for you? Imagine that you want to apply to Jefferson University because you want to become a doctor or a nurse. Would taking a volunteer job at a maternity ward help you land that position? Would visiting the campus and speaking with professors, admissions officers,

and other students give you more insight about the program?

2. If you knew in your heart that a few wisely selected actions could land you in the college of your dreams, why are you not doing them now? What is the price of procrastination? How is putting off your college dreams of tomorrow making you feel *today*?

The Push to Nowhere

Are you stressed out? Do you wake up every morning and go to bed at night with thoughts of failing? Do you feel that you do not have the time to do the things you love or the things you need to do to operate at your best? Do you tell yourself that you cannot read for pleasure because you are too busy cramming for exams? Stop worrying about getting things done quickly. It's not your fault! We have all been programmed in this society to believe that being *faster* is better.

Unless you are careful, cramming can become a way of life. The problem with this kind of thinking is that you'll feel you need to cram to get through all of your classes once you're in college. As coursework and expectations become more intense, your stress level will rise accordingly. Rushing artificially creates a sense of importance, power, and a false sense of accomplishment.

Keep in mind that the purpose of college is more than gaining prestige, titles, respect, recognition, a distinguished career, and a boatload of money. It is also about personal growth and development. College is about networking, making friends, and learning how to learn. Your ultimate success in college is more than getting a job. It is about becoming a better person.

Categories of Daily Activities

To plan the most effective and efficient ways to get into college, recognize that not all activities are created equal.

Quadrant 1 Activities: Urgent and Important

If you have a statement of purpose that is due in three weeks, turn it in immediately. If you are seeking letters of recommendation from professors, ask for them as soon as possible. Otherwise, those tasks will become urgent. You don't want to put out fires throughout your college career. You don't want to be in the Panic Zone.

Quadrant 2 Activities: Important but Not Urgent

Reading for pleasure is a Quadrant 2 activity because it will help you develop analytic and language skills that will help you ace standardized tests that will serve you well after you graduate from college, if not before.

Quadrant 3 Activities: Not Important but Urgent

Browsing your email every two minutes may seem like an important activity, but it is not. There is nothing wrong with this activity, per se. However, it may be a problem if you are spending more time checking your email instead of planning for college.

Quadrant 4 Activities: Not Urgent and Not Important

Watching hours of mindless television shows, gossiping, playing games on your mobile device are examples of quadrant 4 activities. There's nothing wrong with watching a little bit of television or playing a few games. Just make sure these activities do not rob your day. If you are not completing your homework or finding time to read books on the side, find out how many of your activities are in Quadrant 4. If you start to budget your time, you'll have more time to do the things you love and the things you must do to get the things you want. To achieve your goal of getting into the college of your choice, you want to spend most of your time in Quadrant 2. You also want to schedule in time to exercise, meditate, read, and be with loved ones. Remember that college planning includes everything about you.

What if I have a Quadrant 1 Major?

Let's face it: some programs are rigorous, time-consuming, and potentially stressful. Some people love intensity. If you have chosen a major in which all of your activities are urgent and important, it is all the more reason why you need to carefully monitor your time and make sure that everything you do counts. With urgency, reserve time to be relaxed and contemplative so that when you are actively in Quadrant 1, you are calm, focused, and centered.

What if I Encounter Failure?

Like I mentioned earlier, there will be times when you'll meet with temporary defeat. Do not give up. If your plan fails, make a new one. Your ultimate success will not be determined by how many times you fall, but how many times you get up from every fall.

Writing Down Your College Admissions Plans

For you to increase the chances of receiving admissions to the college of your dreams, you must write all of your action steps and schedule them. If you fail to plan, you are planning to fail. Consider the following questions:

- What is most important to me?
- What concrete steps can I take right now that will give me the most meaning in my life?
- Why am I going to college? What do I hope to achieve while I'm in college and beyond its hallowed halls?
- What contributions do I want to make to society?
- Who will I touch?
- How will the world be a better place as a result of the skills I will gain in college and apply them even before I graduate?

Steps to Crafting a Winning, Workable Schedule

Have you ever imagined how much more you would accomplish if you had just a few more hours in a day? Do you ever wonder why some people accomplish many things in 24 hours while others accomplish so little? While it is true that some have more money, support, these are not determining factors in getting things done. Keep in mind that time is the most precious and the most limited resource. Therefore, it is essential to do the most important tasks without expending needless effort. Ditch to-do lists, identify your purpose for college admission, and employ the following techniques to take charge of your time and your life.

1. Brain Dump

Keep a pen and lots of paper, a laptop, a computer or your smartphone by your bed. The moment you awake, write down everything you need to do daily as well as all the action steps to apply for college. Writing down everything important to you is called brain dumping because you will dump on paper everything you need to do. Do not pause and analyze your list. Write them all down.

2. Prioritize

Now that you have this huge laundry list of things to do, it is time for you to categorize your tasks in terms of importance. You want to separate time-sensitive activities from the rest of your duties. Here is how to prioritize:

- Assign a letter to each task from A to E (A being the

highest level activity)
- Spend most of your time doing the most important tasks right away.

For example, if you have a chemistry final in two days, that will have an A value. Studying for your SAT exam may have a B value if you are taking it within a month from now. Separate time-sensitive activities from noncritical activities. For instance, your midterm English literature exam may have a top priority at 9 am when you take it but no value after 6 pm. By tracking and scheduling your activities by priority, you will be surprised how much you can accomplish without the stress of urgency haunting you every moment.

3. *Calendarize*

With the pressure of keeping your grades up, participating in community events, acing your standardized tests, selecting the best college and writing the winning essay, it is easy and understandable that you may feel overwhelmed and forget one seemingly small but significant detail, such as meeting the application deadline which could affect your financial aid, housing and even your chances of gaining admission. Remember that college is a huge undertaking that requires successful planning.

According to Willard Dix in the *Forbes* article, "A Calendar is Your Best Tool in the College Process," **treat every deadline as**

if your life depends on it. Do not fall into the procrastination temptation. Do not assume that you will get an extension, just do it! Keep deadlines at the forefront of your mind with Stephen Covey's "Begin with the end in mind" notion. For example, if the FAFSA deadline is midnight, Central time, June 30, 2019, turn in your FAFSA application early. As you visualize the application date for your application, figure out how many days, weeks, or months, you need to complete it. Mark them on your calendar. Here are some critical items to consider in this process:

- **Ask for Letters of Recommendation Immediately.** Your teachers are human, just like you. They work long hours, have families, and participate in many activities. If you need their endorsement for your college admissions, do not wait until the last minute.
- **Submit Applications Earlier Than the Stated Priority Deadline.** There is an expression that if you are early, you're on time, if you are on time, you are late. These words of wisdom apply to the priority deadlines of the college application.
- **Be on Time by Being Early.** Do not wait until the last minute to complete anything about college admission.

Organized planning is a crucial step in making your college dreams come true because it enables you to consciously create the life you want instead of operating in desperation. You will be able to prioritize all of your work into manageable tasks, complete more quality work in less time and ensure that you are staying on the right track to meet all of your deadlines and your goals for college and beyond. Once you have a plan, it is time to take action. It is time to make a decision toward college admission.

CHAPTER 3

Making the Decision Toward College Admission

Those who reach decisions promptly and definitely, know what they want and generally get it.
Napoleon Hill.

While desire can kindle your college admission passion, procrastination can quickly extinguish it. According to Napoleon Hill, an analysis of more than 25,000 men and women who experienced failure revealed that their inability to make a decision is the main reason they failed in at least 30 major areas in life (Hill, ch.1). He says, "People who fail...without exception, have the habit of reaching decisions, if at all, very slowly..and changing these decisions quickly and often" (Hill, ch. 8).

Many erroneously believe that college is a rite of passage for everyone who graduates from high school. The problem with this ideology is that it is a formula for failure. There are deadlines to submit applications. You will need to get letters of recommendation from teachers, employers, and directors of any volunteer organizations you served in high school or elsewhere. It takes time to contact people. It takes time for professors, supervisors, and mentors to write quality letters of recommendation. Although I have mentioned this point a few times in the book, it is well worth mentioning again: *don't delay.* Reach out to people as soon as possible. Do not wait until the last minute. Remember that teachers and employers are human beings. They are obligated to other students, their families, and other causes. If you wait too late, you may not be able to reach them.

There are deadlines to take standardized admissions exams like the SAT and the ACT. Know what they are and plan accordingly. You will also need to familiarize yourself with the curriculum, culture, living arrangements, and logistics of a few targeted universities. If you dawdle in planning, you will miss critical deadlines, and consequently, you will sabotage your efforts.

My Personal Story of College Decision

Before I graduated from a community college, I was determined to go to UC Berkeley when a recruiter serendipitously came to Sacramento City College. Since I needed to attend a college that was academically challenging and located within the urban community in the Bay Area, I decided that UC Berkeley was the only college for me. I imagined the acceptance letter in my hand, welcoming me to UC Berkeley's college of letters and science.

Even though I did not own a car at that time, my drive to arrive at UC Berkeley was unstoppable. Friends and neighbors in Sacramento drove me to Berkeley so that I could submit all of my paperwork. I asked everyone I knew to take me to orientations and meetings with counselors. When I applied for housing and financial aid, I delivered every document and form to the admissions office to ensure they received all of my paperwork on time.

When I wrote my statement of purpose, I asked the admissions officers in person how I could describe everything about myself on two pages. He told me to reduce the font size, so everything fits on one page. I admit, this was an unorthodox approach, but I learned from experience that you must ask for what you want.

What Will You Become?

Remember that one of the main benefits of going to college is developing into a better version of yourself. Make a list of all the things you want to accomplish. Who do you want to serve? Will you be working with the legislator of your state to protect the environment for your children? Do you wish to chair an environmental committee to clean up toxic refuge in your area? What are your immediate goals on campus?

While planning for college, do not leave your personal life in the dust. Your personhood is not separate from your academic and vocational emerging self. In chapter 2, I emphasized the importance of scheduling in planning for college admission. But keep in mind that college is just one part of your life. Make sure you schedule every part of your activities, including friends, family, and hobbies. Ask yourself, "Do I arrange a time to be spontaneous? Do I include loved ones in my decisions toward college admission?" If you neglect other important areas of your life, every part of your life will be affected. According to Harv Eker. "How you do anything is how you do everything." *The Secrets of the Millionaire Mind.*

College can be very intense at times. Adjusting to campus life can seem overwhelming, but you can do it! Remember, as you learn to master the college environment, you are also learning to master yourself, so be gentle with yourself. Do not be afraid to make changes if some of your plans are not working. Whenever you feel doubts about your decision toward college admission, ask yourself: "What skills will I learn in college that I may not learn elsewhere? How will my relationships improve? What career opportunities will I achieve?"

The Importance of Setting Goals

Keep in mind that goals, like the foundation of a house, structure your future. Without the grounding of goals, your chances of success in college, or life in general, are next to nothing. According to Brian Tracy, a public speaker, and self-development author, "An average person who develops the habit of setting clear priorities and getting important tasks completed quickly will run circles around a genius who talks a lot and makes wonderful plans but who gets very little done" (Tracy, Intro). In other words, dreaming of success is not enough. You must commit your goals to paper.

S.M.A.R.T. GOALS

Make sure that your goals are SMART (Specific, Measurable, Achievable, Realistic, and Time- Bound). S.M.A.R.T is a mnemonic/acronym for criteria to guide in the setting of objectives such as losing weight, winning the debate team, or completing a college degree. Here is a brief description of S.M.A.R.T goals:

Specific

Specific Goals are clear, well defined, measurable, and understandable to anyone who knows the project. A specific goal contains the following:

Where will this take place?

Identify the name and location of your chosen college.

What exactly do I need to accomplish?

I must apply to a few select colleges.

Who else will be involved?

Applying to the college of your choice is not a solo activity. Many will share in your college journey. If you are a high school student, your parents, guidance counselors, teachers, and friends may provide advice, guidance, and financial support. If you are a reentry student, your significant other, employers, business partners, and designated mentors will be part of your team.

Why do you need to accomplish this goal?

Why must you go to college? Will college provide you with the training and credentials for an exciting and fulfilling career path? Will you earn more money for yourself and your family? Is college the vehicle to fulfill your mission to serve others? Will college help you to leave a legacy for your family and future generations?

Measurable

A measurable goal is an ambition, aspiration, or intention that you can measure with numbers.

How will you measure your progress?

- Create a checklist of all the necessary tasks that you need to complete.

- Assign a due date for each action item.
- Prioritize each item by the due date.
- Track your progress. Remember to reward yourself after completing a set of tasks.

A goal is just a dream until you assign a date and take action steps to complete that goal.

For example, let's suppose your goal is to get into Jefferson University, your dream school. Until you target a specific admission date and take all of the necessary steps to complete your application, it is just a dream.

You will know that you accomplished your goals when you can cross out all of the completed items on your checklist by the due dates. When you make goal setting a habit, you will develop the confidence and skills to achieve anything you want.

Achievable

You should strive for a goal that you know you can accomplish. If you set an outrageous goal that you know that you can never achieve, you will feel like you failed. Consequently, it may be hard to feel motivated to set new goals.

You should understand that getting into college is an achievable goal, even if you feel doubtful.

Take one small step at a time each day to applying to the college of your dreams. Keep your checklist of college admission steps handy. Focus on completing one item at a time.

Remember that no one accomplishes anything worthwhile alone. Include your family, friends, instructors, or anyone who has your best interest in mind to support you in getting into the college of your dreams.

Realistic

Your goals should be within the range of resources, knowledge, and time allowable. When plotting your college admissions, realistically assess your capabilities, interests, your budget, and support system from family, friends, and the college of your choice. Being realistic and daring to dream big are not mutually exclusive and should not inhibit you from doing something great. Know your capabilities to expand your abilities. You will be amazed to discover that you can accomplish more than you ever thought you could.

Time-Bound

Now that you have a specific, measurable, achievable, and realistic goal, add a deadline to your goal and stick to it no matter what! Deadlines keep you from tossing and turning in a sea of confusion and never arriving at any destination.

There should be enough time to complete the goal within a specific time frame. For example, if you are accepted to First Choice college in January 2020, earning an undergraduate degree in 2023 is a reasonable time. Watch out for procrastination! It is easy to put off tasks. Be careful! Spending excessive time to finish a project can impact your performance, costs, and outcome of your goals.

Applying the 80/20 rule is another way of managing your time in preparing to get into the college of your choice. It is also known as the Pareto Principle, named after the Italian economist Vilfredo Pareto.

The **80/20 rule** asserts that 80 percent of outcomes are the result of 20 percent of activities for a given event. In other words, 80 percent of your grades and success in college is the results of 20 percent of select actions. Brian Tracy states in *Eat That Frog*, you may have ten tasks to do. Each of those tasks requires the same amount of time to complete each one. However, two of those tasks will contribute five or ten times the value of all of them (Tracy, ch. 3). Concentrate on select activities for college admission that will bring the best results. Gather information from teachers and other faculty to research to get into the college of your choice. They will be more than happy to help you because you are taking action and not sitting on the sidelines. Then you need to select the best activities, prioritize them by deadlines.

A Match Made in Heaven

You want to put your best foot forward in your application and statement of purpose to your select college. Understand that the admissions faculty will evaluate you on a personal as well as on an academic level. It is tempting for students to feel that colleges have the upper hand. In reality, you have a lot of power as an applicant. You can accept or reject an offer just as the college of your choice can accept or reject you. Remember that! Be clear about your values and expectations regarding what a university should deliver for you before you accept an offer. I worked with a student with a 4.7 GPA. He received many offers from several medical schools. However, he rejected an offer because he did not like the school's location nor the ideals of this particular school. Do not feel you have to accept every offer. You have a right to say no. Humans are like plants. They grow at their best when they take root in the right environment. Plant yourself at the college that is right for you.

    Take a piece of paper right now and write down all the resources that will help you get into the college of your dreams. What can you do to increase your likeliness of admission? What courses have you taken, or what volunteer positions have you served that would appeal to an admissions officer? Did you thoroughly research faculty, clubs? What is the vision and mission of this university? Do your values, aspirations, academic, and vocational interests align? Decide what skills, resources, and support you need right now—today—to make college happen. Develop a growth mindset. Carol Dweck, PhD., is one of the leading researchers in the field of motivation and author of Mindset: The New Psychology of Success. She believes that people can have either a fixed or growth mindset. Dweck states that the "growth mindset is based on the belief that your basic qualities are things you can cultivate through your efforts, your strategies, and help from others" (Dweck 6). Dweck maintains that people with a fixed mindset, however believe that their qualities are "fixed in stone." "The fixed mindset—creates an urgency to prove to yourself over and over. If you have a certain amount of intelligence, a certain possibility, and a certain moral character—well, then you'd better prove that you have a healthy dose of them" (6). The reason why those with a fixed mindset feel desperate is because they feel their intelligence or abilities are fixed traits and cannot be changed. Someone who struggles with math will say, "I am not a numbers person" if he or she has a fixed mindset. A person with a growth mindset believes they can improve in areas where they struggle. I encourage you to embrace a growth mindset. Instead of seeing your challenges as pitfalls, look at them as opportunities to grow. Regardless of what happens, do not run away from your goals until you see them through. Take full responsibility for the outcome of your college preparation. Regardless of the economy or the competition, you can decide to study, research the college of your choice, and connect with the right people to help you. The results of your college outcome for tomorrow are determined by your preparation today.

    Do not worry about making mistakes along your college journey. Mistakes are part of learning. Learn from them and move on!

If your personal and college goals do not stand up to the litmus test of these questions, redefine your goals until they do. No matter what you do, do not set your expectations low. Do not hide behind the curtain of fear. Address your negative chatter and the dream bashers who attempt to sabotage your college goals.

When I was attending a community college, a counselor tried to encourage me to take the minimum number of classes to qualify for a state college. I did not compromise. I knew that I wanted to go to UC Berkeley, and so I did. I learned that even well-meaning friends, family, and experts do not always know what is best for you—only you do! The way you assess and determine what is best is to be prepared. Self-preparation is like fueling up at a gas station for a trip. Keep in mind that you are ultimately responsible for your education. Guidance counselors are guides, not gods. Trust, but verify all advice. Don't leave anything to chance.

The college of your dreams is within your reach. When you decide to go to college, set measurable goals, and take reasonable action steps. When you feel doubt about your college dreams, think about why you want to go to college. Think about the skills you will learn, your career prospects, and the people you will touch on your college journey. Remember that during your college planning, obstacles are opportunities. Now, it is time to have faith to keep the fire of college admission passion bright when winter comes.

CHAPTER 4

Faith–The Mighty Thought Force of College Admission

Whatever the mind. . .can conceive and believe, it can achieve."
Napoleon Hill.

Alchemy of Faith

Faith is one of the most powerful emotions on this planet. Faith mixed with desire, definiteness of purpose, and persistence will make you unstoppable!

Repetition is the mother of college admission. When you repeatedly tell your subconscious mind over and over again that you will obtain the college of your choice, you increase your chances of admission. When you first confront the realization that possessing faith is the only way you will succeed academically, your natural impulse is to resist. Do not fight your resistance. Resistance means CHANGE!

When you tell yourself repeatedly that you are worthy of college admission, your protective mind will become accustomed to your new, empowering belief. If your self-doubting self remains in contact with a firm belief in college admission, it will finally embrace it and become influenced by it and succumb.

Winter of Opportunity

In February of 1978, during one of the coldest winters in New York City, I lived in a dorm that was dilapidated. However, I dreamed that someday, I would earn a college degree and live an abundant life. Even though I could not formally complete high school, I went to an adult school and earned my GED in California. Then a counselor advised me to enroll at a community college. I found tutors on campus to help me. I also met with many academic advisors.

Some advisors were very supportive. I spent many years to complete all of my classes, but I eventually earned acceptance to UC Berkeley because I had faith. I knew in my heart that I would find the right people to help me achieve my dream. Today, I help many students of all ages and backgrounds earn their college degrees. I possessed the faith that I would find the resources to make my college dreams possible. It is "faith" that will bring you toward your goals even in the darkest days of winter.

Winter always happens, but spring eventually follows the winter. Don't linger in the cold, dark moments of self-doubt. You can see your dreams materialize in your mind even before you achieve them in reality. Confidence, preparation, and faith made applying and receiving admittance to my dream school a reality. The same thing could happen for you—there is no stopping you!

However, we have been programmed by family and by society to doubt ourselves. Instead of buying into the default negative thinking mode, confront your mental chatter. It is natural and understandable if you feel bombarded with negative thoughts and doubts about your ability to obtain the college of your dreams.

Most of us struggle with trying to keep our wildly negative thoughts corralled. Raj Raghunathan, Ph.D. states that "even though many people desperately need to feel in control of their lives, their negative mental chatter dominates 70% of all their thoughts." Trying to replace negative thoughts with positive ones may work in the short run. However, it may prove to be counterproductive, for we are wired to be on guard since prehistoric times to avoid dangerous predators (How Negative).

Humans naturally think negatively. Adam Hansen is an innovation expert and co-author of *Outsmart Your Instincts*. He says, "Negativity is contagious for evolutionary purposes. When one gazelle in the herd at the watering hole sees a lion, they all see the lion as the recognition spreads like a tidal wave. Those not paying attention get eaten." (Hansen 18)."Therefore, recognize that your self-doubts are not flaws; they are a natural part of your humanity. Instead of trying to make enemies with your negative mind, embrace it as if it were a long lost relative, welcoming faith in your college success.

The Antidote for the Protective Mind

Does your mind often tell you that you cannot fulfill your mission of college admission? Does it tell you that you are not smart enough to attend an Ivy League college? Do you believe that you are unworthy to receive scholarships or financial aid to finance your college dreams? Are you afraid that you will not attract the right people to collaborate with you in making your college dreams come true? Is your mind trying to bully you into abandoning your pursuit of college?

The solution is to quiet your monkey mind. Your monkey mind is that unsettling wild, confused and erratic side of you. Don't fight it! Say to your negative voices: "Thank you for sharing, but I am busy right now fulfilling my mission."

Suspend, Transcend and Ascend

When the negative voices call out to you in the middle of the night, you want to **suspend** those negative thoughts, **transcend** the challenges you face, and **ascend** to evolve into the best version of yourself. Replace all the negative doubts about college admission with positive ones such as, what benefits could come out of attending college? What potential are you starting to see because you are not dismissing the possibilities that a college education will bring you?

To identify your major field of interest and attract the college of your dreams, you must convince your subconscious mind that college is real. Rather than trying to tame your negative monkey mind, embrace the possibility that you are the chosen one of the admissions committee. Allow your faith to make all of your thoughts crackle with confidence and push you toward limitless heights in self-development and accomplishments.

No Such Thinking as Random Misfortune

Do you often ask yourself: What if I fail my final exams? What if I am not accepted? What if I get into the college of my dreams and fail? If any of this unsubstantiated but seemingly clear and present mental chatter clutters your college goals, you are not alone! Millions believe they have no control over their lives. They are forgers of their negative beliefs, manufacturers of outrageous misfortune. Consequently, the subconscious mind picks up the signals of negativity and translates them into their physical counterparts.

Keep in mind that all of those random negative thoughts are just the natural workings of your critical mind. They are not grounded in reality. Your ultimate success in this life is not solely dependent on a test or the board room of a college admissions committee. To stop those negative imaginings from dominating your life, deceive yourself by believing you are already successful.

Faith Empowers the Mind

Many religions insist that vulnerable humans embrace faith without showing others how to have faith. As a result, many dismiss faith as a fanciful whim. However, it is the only known antidote to failure and the starting point of transforming your college admission dreams into reality, according to Napoleon Hill.

Once you implant the unstoppable belief that you are college worthy, you will produce a magnetic force that will launch a chain reaction of similar thoughts of success. When you begin to radiate with confidence, you will attract other people, discover resources, and breakthrough the dry grounds of the college admission process.

To open the college admission doors of possibilities, resolve to cast aside any negative influences, especially those who encourage you to abandon your dreams. Embrace your strengths. Find the self-confidence within by following these steps:

1. Insist that you will believe in yourself and take action toward your college dreams.
2. Hold in your mind the constant belief that college is possible.
3. Remember that constant thoughts transform themselves into reality. Keep positive thoughts of college admission close at hand.
4. Revisit your mission statement and keep in mind

your chief aim in life and how a college education will enable you to fulfill that aim.
5. Be true to yourself and others as you develop academically. Engage in no activity that inhibits your self-development.

Avoid the Dark Zone

Just as fire can cook a meal or light up a room, it could also burn down a house. Your thoughts are an electrical powerhouse of incalculable abilities. You can dream big or travel down the dark rabbit hole of doubt and discouragement. Although the gloomier dimensions of thought may seem unstoppable, you have the power to embrace the bright, white light of college success.

Affirming that you deserve to get into the college of your dreams, even by chanting positive affirmations may feel daunting at first. Therefore, entrust the support of a mentor. If your emotional bank account is running low on faith, a mentor is a compass to guide you to your true north. Audit classes and pretend you will receive a letter grade for them.

Before addressing some of the concrete steps to planning for college admission, consider the following quote from Napoleon Hill:
"If you *think* you are beaten you are,
If you *think* you dare not, you don't, If
you like to win, but you think you can't, It

is almost certain you won't. If you *think*
you'll lose, you're lost
For out of the world we find, Success begins with a person's will—
It's all in the *state of mind*.
If you *think* you are outclassed, you are,
You've got to *think* high to rise,
You've got to be sure of *yourself* before you can ever win a prize.
Life's battles don't always go
To the stronger or faster man
But soon or late, the man who wins
Is the man WHO THINKS HE CAN!" (Hill 55)

  College admission begins as a thought. Make your subconscious mind work on your college dreams. Find a quiet spot before you go to bed. Then say, "I am capable. I am hard-working, and I will get into the college of my choice."

  Assign a date that you will receive admission to the college of your choice. Create a vision board. Take a picture of the college of your choice.

  Faith is the driving force that will make college admission dreams happen. Though people believe they are rational, practical beings, they are driven by their emotions, mostly negative ones. Refuse to choose self-doubt. Believe! By daring to dream, your dream school may happen. As you will discover in the next chapter, your passion will be your practical guiding force in selecting the best field of study in college.

CHAPTER 5

The Practicality of Passion in Choosing a Major

Do what you love. Know your own bone; gnaw at it, bury it, unearth it, and gnaw it still.
Henry D. Thoreau.

You should applaud yourself for making the difficult decision to attend college. College today is incredibly diverse. Students of all ages and socio-economic backgrounds are applying to college in record numbers. Many enter college after a layoff. Some are returning to college several years later. Many, however, do not recognize the diversity of the new college environment.

When you tell others that you are going to college, do some well-meaning individuals ask, "Why are you going to college? What is your major? Will you get a job? How can you go to college at your ripe old age?" Do these kinds of questions make you feel pressured? Does the commentary from others derail you and make it hard for you to enjoy the college journey?

Do you feel that if you choose a major, you are stuck with it for the rest of your life? I have great news for you! Do not worry that you will waste thousands of dollars, priceless years, and many sleepless nights preparing for one career that you will hate for the rest of your life.

When I decided to go to college in my 20s, I was not only seeking the right field of study, and the perfect career, I was hoping to find the self esteem I never had. At 15, I ran away from home to escape an abusive environment and became homeless in New York. Even though I often did not have enough food to eat or certainty about where I would sleep on any given night, I survived on the hope that I would one day go to college, obtain a fabulous education and live the American dream. However, since I bounced from place to place, I never finished high school. I needed support, direction, and guidance. Unfortunately, I was looking for advice in all the wrong places. At an adult school, a counselor told me that I needed to live in the real world because I could not afford to go to school full time.

Nevertheless, I completed my GED. I did not allow my age or the opinion of others to stop me from enrolling at a community college. My hard work and perseverance eventually paid off! I earned admission to UC Berkeley. I graduated with a degree in English. With a college degree, I have been able to guide other students in their academic journey. Still, I understand that getting into the college of your choice is challenging at best.

Landing a major is even more daunting. Realize that many will try to persuade you to choose a field they think is practical and lucrative. However, there is no guarantee that the career you are studying for today will exist when you graduate from college. About 80% of students will change their major at least once. Many students, on average, change their major at least three times (Borderzine 2019). Understand that it is okay to change your major. As you acquire more education and increase your network, you will discover more choices. You will no longer work at one company for 40 years to get a gold watch. In this age of technological advances, expect to change careers at least three to five times. When you job-hunt more often, you get good at branding yourself. You will know what the market wants because you are in the market more frequently. You will know how to brand yourself and pick up new procedures, protocols, strategies, and other invaluable talents (Ryan 2016). Keep in mind that whether you work for someone or yourself, you are an entrepreneur. If your major in college or a job is not working, change it. Change or be a victim of change: the choice is yours.

Ultimately, it is up to you to decide which major to pursue. Be that as it may, there are some critical points to ponder.

Consider Online Degree Programs

The traditional, brick-and-mortar colleges are not the only way to obtain an advanced degree and job training. Online colleges have made a college education more available than ever. From the comfort of home, you can earn a degree while balancing the demands of family, work, childcare, and healthcare. Online course materials are available at any time of the day or night. You can control your time and your budget since there are no additional costs for transportation.

Do Your Homework

Make sure that you choose a school with a solid reputation and track record. One of the reasons why I applied to UC Berkeley is because of a scene from the movie, *My Cousin Vinny*. Judge Chamberlain Haller (Fred Gwynne) asks Vinny Gambini (Joe Pesci) where he went to law school. Gambini replies that he went to the Brooklyn Academy of Law. Judge Hallerman asks if that is an accredited law school. I chose UC Berkeley because no one would question its credibility since it is well-recognized as at the top in many departments.

Choose a Major That Interests You

No one can choose your major for you. Parents and spouses may focus on particular majors that seem to promise a high income and job security. Colleges pressure you to declare your major during your sophomore year, but you are likely to change your mind. Most of the advice you receive on majors is wrong. For instance, many believe that they will earn big money if they major in science or computer programming. However, not everyone in these fields makes it to the top of the pay scale. Research these fields carefully. Make sure that you have the passion and developed reasonable mastery in these areas before committing to them. When choosing a major, consider the following options:

Study Subjects that Sharpen Your Mind

Earning high marks is understandably an important consideration in selecting a major and getting into the college of your choice. A transcript with glittering grades opens doors to universities, scholarships, and career options that carry the weight of prestige.

However, it is essential to focus on what grades represent instead of the grades themselves. If you pursue a major you love, do so wholeheartedly with the intent to excel to the highest level of achievement.

Investigate Other Avenues to Obtaining Your Career

Traditionally for many generations, pre-med students had to master organic chemistry, physics, and ace the Medical College Admissions Test, also known by its familiar, ulcer-inducing acronym, the MCAT. However, just as all roads lead to Rome, there are many paths to getting into college. Imagine that your fascination for archeology, history, and poetry or music might be the back door to entering an esteemed college in a practical field. National *New York Times* correspondent, Anemonia Hartocollis, describes how an a cappella singer received admittance at the highly competitive Mount Sinai program on the Upper West Side of Manhattan. She initially would not describe herself as a prime candidate for medical school, even though her father was a physician.

Based on data from the AAMC, humanities majors have roughly the same chance of getting into medical school as that of physical sciences, which is around 46-48% acceptance rate. The reason why humanities majors have a great shot at medical school is that they typically read better and write better. Plus, they engage in broad-range thinking applicable to many disciplines (Hartocollis). Therefore, even if your passion for humanities major seems impractical, it may be your ticket to landing the college of your choice and your career. However, there are other things to keep in mind.

Apply the Lean Startup Principle

Brett Hoffstadt is a dual-degree aerospace engineer with certifications in project management and public speaking and licenses in remote piloting (drones) and insurance sales. He is an inventor with two patents and the author and publisher of four books. He is also an entrepreneur and music composer with one album released.

Brett is a big fan of the **lean startup** methodology. Let's say you have an idea for a product. Before you invest lots of money, time, and risk in building a big company and opening a brick-and-mortar store, what can you do to quickly and inexpensively test your idea? Building a prototype is a possibility. You can place your prebuilt product on a website and ask customers to click a link and preorder it. It does not take long to build a prototype for your product to determine if there is a market for it. Using a prototype is a way for you to ask yourself, "Can I make money with this?" (Hoffstadt).

College students need to take the same approach. Students need to find an institution that appreciates this approach so that they can learn as quickly as possible to find a job in their career. Traditionally, they will wait four years or six years and see what happens in the industry you are pursuing. At the end of this journey, they'll hopefully find a job. If they are lucky, all of those years that they spent and all the money that they have invested will pay off in the long run.

But in today's world, within four to six years, entire industries are born while others die. Consider how impractical it is to spend more time preparing for a career that will be obsolete by the time you graduate. College and universities must adapt to this new world. Brett Hoffstadt likes to share wisdom about how students can test the practicality and economic viability of their intended field of study.

Brett says that students need to protect themselves from this trend of waiting until they graduate before planning their careers. Instead, they should make sure that their school has internships and co-op programs. These programs provide a structured method of combining classroom education workshops at the universities. With a co-op program, you would spend a semester in school and another semester in the workforce. Co-op assignments take place during a regular school semester. On the other hand, an internship is typical during the summer. The engineering program at Drexel University in Philadelphia has a mandatory co-op program requiring you to take classes while working at a company for three or four months. If you have to do this on your own and miss core classes that will not work in your favor, it has to be built into the university framework. The point of this program is that you are getting into the market sooner. It solves the problem of waiting four to six years to get into the industry; you need to get into a college or university that puts you in the industry as soon as possible. The benefit of this program is that it allows you to earn money and to see the trend of the industry while you are still in college. You can take that practical knowledge with you right back into the classroom.

Colleges have not been subject to the same type of market scrutiny as industries. However, since there is so much innovation taking place in industries, universities and colleges must compete with the corporate world. Consequently, they are not set up to provide students with vital life and job skills. In college, few students know how to network, negotiate, and smoothly transition from college to work. Colleges are doing a disservice to graduates by not teaching them real-world skills from the very start. Brett says, "If colleges and universities had to provide a money-back guarantee on the degrees they offer, most of them would go out of business" (Hoffstadt). Colleges cannot guarantee that their graduates will be gainfully employed when they graduate. Many college graduates are unemployed. The ultimate goal is to strike a balance between discovering a career you love that also earns you enough money. Finding a job that is well-paying and satisfying is challenging. The world is dynamic. People change. Industries change. Your skills will change over time as you acquire new ones. However, college does not consider these dynamics. College graduation has been entirely left to chance. The objective of higher education is to gain lots of theoretical knowledge on several general subjects. Then you declare a major intending to land a practical career path. You should pursue a field you love. At the same time, you need to explore the viability of your intended career path. Make sure that you can earn money and that the career you prepare for today will exist tomorrow.

Your Passion May Be Economically Practical

Many students are strongly encouraged to pick majors that they believe will smoothly usher them into a prestigious, lucrative, inflation-resistant jobs. With honorary titles from an elite college, they wrongly believe that employers will come out of the woodwork. Nothing could be further from the truth. A college degree will provide you with a wide range of skills that could be useful on the job.

A college is a great place for personal growth and networking, but it may or may not guarantee you the career of a lifetime. You still need to polish your interpersonal, organizational, and networking skills. Before you graduate, investigate careers that are currently experiencing growth like nursing, allied health professions, and data science. Do your passion and your field of interest align with these trendy jobs? If not, would you be willing to take classes, correspondence courses, or internships to make you competitive?

Keep in mind that just because there are plenty of jobs available within an industry does not guarantee financial stability. For example, there is a desperate need for teachers, but teachers are notoriously underpaid, overworked, and underappreciated. If teaching is your calling, go for it. If you seek high income, a college or university professor might be your calling. Although it pays a lot more, it also requires additional education and degrees like masters or a doctorate.

A Whole New Mind Shift

Many students have been encouraged over the years to pursue traditional, analytic, left-brained careers like engineering, mathematics, computer science, and finance-focused law. Though these careers currently pay well, there is a cultural economic and technical shift occurring at an accelerated pace. Daniel Pink is an author of six provocative books about work and management—four of them are on the *New York Times* bestseller list. In *A Whole New Mind*, Pink calls this rapid sea change the Conceptual Age, where rewards go to the playful and meaningful personalities. On the other hand, many legal, engineering, and programming jobs may disappear in place of automation. According to Pink, people must be able to "create artistic and emotional beauty, craft a satisfying narrative, and to combine seemingly unrelated ideas into something new" (Pink, 2). Jobs that require repetitive actions like computer programming may be the first to go because a robot can do them. On the other hand, empathetic careers like nursing will remain for some time because this profession requires a caring, compassionate bedside manner.

When choosing a major, keep these concepts of Daniel Pink at the forefront of your mind. If you love art, music, or enjoy being with people, your seemly impractical, right-brained career choices may be a logical choice in the long run. According to Pink, our economy has shifted from an economy built on left-brained thinking to right-brained thinking. "It's just no longer sufficient...to survive in this age, individuals and organizations must examine what they are doing to earn a living and ask themselves three questions:

1. Can someone overseas do it cheaper?

2. Can a computer do it faster?
3. Is what I'm offering in demand in an age of abundance?" (Pink 50-51).

We are no longer living in a linear world where high-tech skills alone will command a bright, lucrative future. We need what he calls "high concept and high touch" skills. Your art, music, literature classes may turn out to be the practical choices to earn a living in today's conceptual age.

Choosing a major in college requires that you follow your heart while exploring the economic viability and practical steps to enter your chosen field. Once you have identified a field of interest, you are ready to explore potential colleges to determine if they are the right colleges for you.

CHAPTER 6

Taking the Test Drive

"One important key to success is self-confidence. An important key to self-confidence is preparation."
Arthur Ashe.

Congratulations on deciding on college! You have just made a significant choice that can potentially enrich your friendships, career choices, knowledge, and income. However, please make sure that the college you ultimately choose is genuinely your choice! Avoid the temptation to settle on a college based on parents, peer pressure, rankings in magazines, and the allure of prestige. You need to choose a college that is intellectually stimulating, academically enriching, socially appealing, and in line with your values and your mission.

Justin Bayer, Founder and Chief Executive Officer for the company Welcome to College, understands that a college visit is critical. Justin has more than 12 years of experience in education. He says, "The tour is the most important part because it is the first real connection a student has with the campus. Since so much of the college admissions process is numbers and research, the first real visit is where you can establish real relationships with people at that institution and assess whether that institution is the right fit for you. It is also a way for you to assess the cultural aspects of the university. Since you are going to be in the environment for the next four years, it is essential for you to know that your selected college is the right one for you" (Bayer).

You should schedule many different campus tours throughout the day. Take time to explore the social scene and examine the academic climate of life. While you're there, think about how you feel. Are you happy? Are you comfortable? Also, think about the people around you. Are resources readily available? Is the faculty approachable, informative, and are there possible mentors? Next, think about your surroundings. How close are you to stores, recreation, and public transportation? If you have medical needs, do you have everything you need nearby? Take note of the parking options while onsite. Is parking expensive? Do you need a permit? Think about the parking distance to the classroom buildings and specifically, the classrooms you will be attending.

Even though the demands of college will keep most students studying night and day, remember that the key to doing well in college and life, in general, is achieving balance.

Plan in Advance

Keep in mind that there is a season for everything. This is especially true for college planning and visiting the campus of choice. Make sure that you schedule your visit ideally for two months in advance. You can find all the information regarding campus tours by visiting the campus website. Before visiting the campus, book your itinerary in advance. Find out if there are exclusive travel discounts. For example, Amtrak offers special discounts at certain times. Check into these. If you are traveling by plane, book your trip well in advance so that you get the lowest rate. Research different airlines to find out which ones offer the lowest prices. According to Anna Miller-Tiedeman, President of the New Careering Institute and author of *How Not to Succeed and Make It*, "Transportation is one of the greatest challenges to success in college."

The best time to visit a college is when classes and activities are in session and flooded with students. Fridays are usually great days to attend college only if you want to savor a smorgasbord of weekend activities. To fully appreciate the dynamics of the college environment, it is essential to visit during regular school days during the week. If you live near the campus, visit the library and conduct research on various aspects of the school. If you drive to school daily, take a good look at the parking. How easy is it to find a parking space? How long will it take you to walk from the parking lot to your classes? Is parking expensive? Are there free parking places on nearby streets? If you want to avoid the hassle of driving, can you take public transportation? Is it close to campus? Fridays are great days to visit a campus because you can take advantage of weekend activities. However, administrative offices are not available. There are no classes in session and typically no one to advise or direct you.

Find out when exam weeks occur by visiting the website or contacting the school to avoid scheduling your visit during these times. Avoid visiting campuses during Thanksgiving, Christmas, New Year's, or other significant holidays. It may be possible that you are unable to attend when classes are in session. In that case, take a guided tour. Talk with students, teachers, admissions personnel, and the coordinators of extra-curricular activities. Ask lots of questions. Make appointments to speak with professors in your designated field. Take notes. Schedule an appointment to talk with a professor who might teach a class you plan to take. Develop a relationship with that professor early on. That professor could be a potential reference for graduate school or a career field down the road.

Send an email to college admissions:

Dear Admissions Office,
I am planning on visiting UC Berkeley on September 25th. My

objective is to major in Political Science and to join the California Golden Bears. I have plans to visit Professor Smith at 2:30 PM and Coach Wainwright at 5:00 PM. I would greatly appreciate it if you would send me any relevant information
Sincerely, A Sincere Student

Take the Virtual Tour

Save time and money! Go online! Taking a virtual tour can teach you many things about a college before you take a live tour. Here are some of the many outstanding online resources to help you plan for exams, virtual tour campuses, and make connections with other students:

College Board
www.collegeboard.com

As the leader in generating testing for college admissions, this site provides a plethora of scholarship information, SAT registration and practice tests, financial aid eligibility, and resources to explore colleges.

Set to Go
www.settogo.org

This site has excellent places to pick a school that is right for you and learning ways of managing stress while on campus. Set to Go helps prospective students to consider all the factors of college admission. It will help you to determine which college is the best option for you. Additionally, this site addresses resources to deal with the stress of exams, adopting to campus life, and dealing with depression. This site will help you find the right solution for dealing with emotional obstacles.

College Confidential
www.collegeconfidential.com

As one of the best college search programs on the Web, you can participate in thriving message boards with parents and student participants. You can receive admissions insights and guidance during your academic journey. Also, there are excellent suggestions and advice to prepare you for college and prepare for a wide range of exams throughout your entire college career.

Campus Tours
www.campustours.com

This site is an outstanding, complete, interactive virtual tour guide with campus maps.

Questions to Consider During Visits

Who Will Teach Me?

Learn as much as possible about faculty, who will teach you, evaluate you, and set the tone of your four years. Make sure that you know who teaches the general and upper-division courses. Ask students who they believe are the best teachers and the most approachable. You can even schedule high-level visits with faculty and interview them. Revisit the questions I recommend asking in the 80/20 Rule section of chapter 3.

What Are the College's Strengths and Weaknesses?

When deciding college admission, make a list of the pros and cons of any college you're considering. If the advantages outweigh the disadvantages, then you're likely on the right track.

Do You Feel an Affinity with the Students?

Mark Twain once said, "Good friends, good books, and a sleepy conscience: this is the ideal life." No doubt, you will be exposed to many good books and a few horrible ones in college, whether you welcome them or not. But good friendships need to be cultivated and nurtured for them to blossom. Your relationships and precious memories are priceless! Find out if you and the students share similar values, academic interests, hobbies, and social interests. Ask them about the academic pressures they face, the workload of their assignments, and their opinions about their professors. When you reach out to them, ask yourself questions about your impression of them. Trust your instincts. Do they share your ambitions?

Will they go above and beyond the expectations of their classes? The quality of your friendships primarily determines the quality of your college life. If you believe you have chemistry with your peers, make sure the combination is productive and not destructive.

How is the Social Atmosphere?

College is more than demanding professors and book study and crowded lecture halls—it is an experience that will shape your character and personality for years to come. Look at the many ways that students at your college of choice amuse themselves. Is there an appropriate balance between study, hard work, and play? What is the stance on drugs, dating, and drinking? Where do students tend to congregate after hours? Are there fraternity parties? Do the students seem thoughtful and considerate about what they say? Abraham Lincoln once said, "When I get ready to talk to people, I spend two-thirds of the time thinking [about] what they want to hear and one-third thinking about what I want to say." Do they listen to what *you* say before they tell you about what they want to say?

What is the Physical State of the Campus?

What is the condition of the buildings? Do they appear to be old, worn, and outdated? Is there a new construction on the horizon? New buildings are a sign that the college might be well funded, and new programs and facilities are on the horizon.

Technology

Does your prospective college of choice offer plenty of computers with printing facilities that are state of the art and up to date? Can you quickly obtain a laptop on campus if you do not own a personal computer?

What Are the Classroom Sizes?

Will you be attending large lecture halls with hundreds of other students at one time with classes taught by graduate students? Are there many seminar rooms, suggesting a personal touch and possible one-on-one interaction with professors? When assessing the size, determine if you are the type of student who needs guidance and attention or thrives anonymously among a nameless, faceless group of students.

What is the Style of Instructors?

Take a close look at the way professors present their lessons. Do they depend on overused PowerPoint presentations, or do they personally deliver compelling, engaging lessons with passion and clarity? How does the professor engage the audience? Does he read from worn, torn lecture notes, or does he fully engage all of his students? Is he approachable or arrogantly aloof? Is there an intellectual enthusiasm in the class, or are students enduring the lecture in agonizing boredom? How do you feel?

Investigating several colleges is essential to ensure that the academic, social, and emotional climate matches your temperament, learning style, and social needs. Do not assume that just because a school is prestigious or suitable for your friends, it is ideal for you. Make sure it is right for *you*. When you are clear that the college you have selected meets all of your needs, the next step is preparing to ace the college admission essay discussed in the next chapter.

CHAPTER 7

Virtuoso Interviews for College Admissions

Interviews are vital, but you cannot allow an interview to take your life and disturb it.
Jerry Lewis. (BrainyQuote)

Like the college essay, students dread the thought of the college interview. Relax! Take a deep breath! Take a load off your feet! If the admission gods accepted your essay and invited you to a meeting, your chances of admission are good. You may think, however, that you will blow your chances of getting into your dream school! Recognize that an interview is a two-way process. The colleges are checking you out to make sure you are a good fit for them. At the same time, you are checking them out to make sure they are a good fit for you.

Most colleges do not even require an interview as part of their admission process. Those that do merely want to make sure those who were accepted will enroll.

Before the Interview

Do Your Homework

Before your interview date, make sure you review the mission and vision of your select college. Interview friends, family, and teachers; practice in front of a mirror until you feel confident. Perfect practice makes perfect! Then, research your college to find out the purpose of the conference. Is the intent of the meeting to clarify information in your application? Do your interviewers need to decide if the person you are presenting in front of them matches the person you displayed on paper? Prepare a list of interview questions that the admissions officers might ask. Also, find out if one, two, or a whole panel of interviewers will interview you. Where will your interview take place? Will it occur on campus? Will you meet with a college alumnus in your home area? Preparedness is the key that will unlock doors to future employment and provide you with the confidence to impress an interviewer.

Prepare to Answer the Following Questions:

Tell Me About Your School or Academic Subject

Think carefully about your response before answering

these questions. You want to come across as investigative, thoughtful to the opinions of others, and sensitive to how your experiences will contribute to the academic community of your select college.

What Is Your Favorite Book?

Try to avoid mentioning books that are commonly assigned in high school unless your analysis is original and thought-provoking.

Why Do You Want to Enroll Here?

Again, do your homework! Learn about your college's unique mission and vision. Know about the college's unique programs and resources specific to that college. If you do all of these things, you will ace this question. The trick is to incorporate your sincere interests with the things that the college wants to promote. Always keep in mind that any questions asked about your benefits and personal challenges are never about you. They are about the college you are applying to and how you will make that college look good.

How Do You Explain Your Dip in Academic Performance?

Mention any gap in your academic records such as excessive absences or low grades. Do not hold back any questionable information about your educational history. Now is the time to tell your story and appeal to your humanity. If you have a learning disability that impacts your concentration, say so. Make sure you have a copy of your transcript so that you can demonstrate where you experienced difficulty and how you feel you have progressed. An occasional dip in performance is not necessarily a disqualifier. Admission officers are impressed with students who show how they grew as a result of poor grades and how they converted their failures into success. The whole purpose of the interview, as well as the essay, is to reveal things that are not apparent in grades and standardized test scores. Get used to meeting with many people in formal and informal settings—polish your presentation skills for possible jobs, a business, or to meet a special someone.

What Other Colleges Have You Considered?

How you address this loaded question will make you or break you in the interview. If you have done your homework on each school you applied to, the interviewer will be impressed with your knowledge. Explain how each college is similar and different from your select school, and why you feel your preferred college is the right one for you.

Dress for Success

Dress comfortably, but nicely. You will not need to don a three-piece suit with a starched white shirt and tie, but you also should not show up looking like you just rolled out of bed. Even though the interview will most likely be an informal meeting, you still want to dress to impress. Keep in mind that most people make their first impressions about what type of person you are within the first five minutes. Your objective in the interview is to appear calm, composed, yet well-groomed and confident.

Arrive on Time

You must show up on time for your appointment. Arrive 15 minutes early! There is a saying, "If you're early, you're on time. If you're on time, you are late." When traveling to your interview, expect the unexpected. Keep Murphy's Law always at the forefront of your mind: "What can go wrong, will." Plan for traffic jams, accidents, and the "unlikely" possibility that the shirt you threw in the dryer the night before, did not dry. Make sure you know the directions to and from the location of the interview. Write them on a sheet of paper, just in case the GPS in your car or on your mobile device malfunctions. Arriving on time, not only shows respect for the busyness of others, it sets the tone for how you plan to show up for life. Woody Allen says, "Eighty percent of success is showing up."

Observe the Nonverbal Cues

Dr. Albert Mehrabian, a pioneer researcher in body language, claims that around 55% of all communication is made up of body language, 38% is the tone of voice, and only 7% is nonverbal (Pease). When you first meet with your interviewer, give a firm, but not a bone-crushing handshake. Your handshake is one of those nonverbal forms of communication that instantly tells someone your level of warmth and confidence. After you exchange a few pleasantries, be sure to maintain eye contact, be responsive, listen intently, and be fully present. Sit down comfortably in your chair. Do not cross your arms. Doing so usually means that you are conveying that you are either not interested in what the other person is saying or that you feel defensive or insecure. Avoid the temptation to talk during the entire interview continuously. Keep in mind that communication is about listening and sharing. Watch for subtle cues. Discern when to speak and when to listen. If your interviewer tends to be a talker, display active listening by nodding at the appropriate times and repeating key points of the interviewer in your own words.

As I mentioned previously in this chapter, the interview is a two-way street. Think of the interview as a date. The interviewer is checking you out to see if you are an excellent candidate to promote the image of your select college. At the same time, you are checking out the college to determine if you want to spend a few years of your life at this particular school. Don't believe that the interviewer has more power over you. You are also screening the potential college to find out if it is right for you. Make sure you do not ask any questions that you can find answers to by browsing the college's website.

Questions To Ask Your Interviewer

What Internships Are Available?

Find out the evaluation process for internships, its length of time, and what a typical workday looks like for a program specific to your college major. Ask questions about mentorship and support you will receive throughout the internship. Internships are not necessarily required to complete college. However, most graduate programs look for an internship experience. Completing apprenticeship demonstrates a student's sincere interest in a potential career field. Plus, future employers look favorably on those willing to intern.

An internship allows the student flexibility to learn about the industry and decide if this is the right area for you without other factors to consider as you would being an employee of a company.

What Values Do You Want to Impart on Your Student Body?

Ask about distinct ideals that this college holds as sacred. For example, Jefferson University's medical program values compassion and empathy.

What Are the Most Common Career Avenues for Graduates?

Find out if the student body at your select school has similar career aspirations and how they should prepare to enter the world of work. Are most students usually employed immediately after graduation, or do most take several months off to travel?

How Do You Support Students in Preparing for a Career in Their Major?

Determine if you will receive lots of guidance and resources to either pursue graduate school or a career. Is there a career center? How do they help students find work or the best graduate school for their academic interests?

After the Interview

Write a Thank-You Letter

You must write a thank-you letter to acknowledge the people who interviewed you immediately after the interview. A note of acknowledgment will make you stand out among competing students for the following reasons:

- Spotlight your best qualities
- An opportunity to mention things not addressed in the interview
- Provide examples of how you will contribute significantly to the college's academic community
- Help the interviewer strongly consider you by showing your follow-through and zeal.

Do not write a long thank-you letter, but do not write one that is too short. A letter of appreciation should be no more than one page.

Snail Mail or Email

While sending snail mail and regular mail are a matter of choice, sending email letters has the following advantages:
- Email can be sent instantaneously within minutes of an interview
- Including attachments, links and other relevant information is possible.

Though email is fast, efficient, and convenient, send a follow-up, hand-written letter to add a personal, second touch.

Here is an example of a thank-you letter:

Dear Interviewer:

Thank you so much for taking the time out of your busy day to meet with me about enrolling as a student at _____ college/university. I particularly found our talk about The Collaborative Faculty Apprenticeship fascinating. Not only can students work directly with a distinguished professor, but they can also gain extracurricular work at a global level. I have reviewed the work of Professor Higgins and find his work fascinating. Also, as I mentioned, I have worked for six months with the latest in bioinformatics in healthcare. Under the direction of Dr. Smith at the National Cancer Institute, I learned about the early treatment of cancer using CRISPR in detecting Lyme disease. I am open to future discussions about additional programs, internships, and courses.

Again, thank you for your consideration and time.
With Appreciation, Brian South

After you write the thank-you letter, celebrate! Go out to dinner, take a drive, or do something relaxing! Getting an interview is a huge accomplishment. Then relax! Allow your mind to clear before applying to another college.

If the college of your choice requires an interview as part of the admissions process, you must research and practice interview questions until you feel comfortable. Interviewing is a life-long skill that you will use to get into college and obtain employment. Knowing how to interact with others will serve you well, especially when you need to reach out to faculty and employers to endorse you. It is now time to learn how to get excellent letters of recommendation from faculty and employers.

CHAPTER 8

The Importance of Obtaining Great Letters of Recommendation

It's not what you know; it's about who recommends you.
Brian South.

Letters of recommendation are not only critical for admission to the college of your choice, but they can also impact your employability and ability to obtain internships. Being a topnotch scholar and leader in student government may not be enough to land you that coveted seat in a college. You need validation from credible people who know you, like you, and can legitimately vouch for your character, work ethics, dedication, and academic performance. Robert B. Cialdini, Ph.D. says, "We are trained from birth that obedience to proper authority is right, and disobedience is wrong." *Psychology of Influence* (Cialdini

218). In other words, people will instinctively believe that you are probably talented, hard-working, and reliable if an authority figure, like a professor, is willing to vouch for you.

Who is a Good Candidate for a Letter of Recommendation?

Do not make the mistake of padding your application with dozens of letters of recommendation from faculty who barely know you, your employer at a fast-food joint, or your next-door neighbor. A great letter of recommendation should come from a teacher, counselor, internship director, or an employer, directly affiliated with your chosen field or major study. And, for goodness sake, make sure that the recommender knows you. If you are in high school, try to get teachers from challenging courses you have taken around your junior or senior year. It is best to find a teacher who appreciates your deeper, less apparent qualities while validating your academic accomplishments and work ethic.

When Should I Ask for a Letter of Recommendation?

Long before the application deadline, students should request letters of recommendation from their teachers. The more time you allow, the stronger the recommendations will be. It is challenging to expect a quality letter from a teacher rushed at the last minute. Besides, it is common courtesy to respect your teacher's time. Remember that teachers are human, just like you. They have families, hobbies, and many obligations besides teaching a seminar. Thrusting one more task on them at the spur of the moment is not the best way to win friends and influence admissions officers.

Furthermore, some teachers will only write so many recommendations per year. If you do not seize them while the iron is hot, you may miss the opportunity forever. Given the competitive nature of college admission, that one outstanding letter from your teacher could be the difference between acceptance and rejection. Ask now. Do not delay. Whenever you begin a course, plant a seed in your instructor's mind that one day, you may ask that teacher for a letter of recommendation. The way you can do this is to develop a relationship with the teacher as soon as possible. Sit in the front row. Visit the teacher often during office hours. Ask intelligent questions related to the subject you are studying. Learn more about the teacher's personal qualities, habits, interests.

What Information Should I Supply My Recommenders?

Ask for a letter of recommendation, ask in person. Provide specific papers that the teacher highlighted as exceptional résumés. Explain to your teacher what college you are applying to, why you are applying to that particular college, and what points you would like your teacher to emphasize. A word to the wise: save all papers that you have turned into your instructors, especially graded ones. Your essays and other submitted work will be an easy reference for your instructor to recall your outstanding qualities and contributions.

How to Make a Request

I highly recommend that you make your recommendation face to face. Do not ask for a letter during class time. Preferably, schedule a private meeting during office hours. Though asking for a letter of recommendation may feel scary, keep in mind that most teachers want and expect this. Believe it or not, it is part of their job to recommend students. As long as you perform at your highest, display tenacity, determination, and an impeccable work ethic, you should feel great about asking for a letter. If you feel like your mouth is full of marbles when you approach your teacher, here is a possible way you can ask:

"I enjoyed your class. I learned many things and grew tremendously as a person and as a student because of your influence. I would feel honored and much obliged if you could write me a strong letter of recommendation for my college application."

Remember that you want your teacher to write you a STRONG RECOMMENDATION, not a generic one. If your teacher declines or seems hesitant, thank your teacher and move on. Do not take your teacher's refusal personally. If you fear rejection, do a sales job. Place yourself in situations where people say "no" so often you become desensitized to rejection and even welcome it, knowing that every "no" in life brings you that much closer to a "yes." Throughout your life, you will need to make many requests for many things. Not everyone will agree with you. When asking for jobs, internships, or colleges in this life, take the attitude that some will, some won't, who cares!

The Logistics of the Recommendation

Let your teachers known your deadlines. As discussed later, your early decision deadlines will be in October, and your regular decisions for college admission will occur in early January. They will typically upload their letters through the Common Application or Naviance (www.naviance.com) if your school uses that platform.

How Should You Ask for a Letter of Recommendation from Your School Counselor?

Practically every single college you apply to will want at least one of your letters from your school counselor referred to as a "secondary school report." Make no mistake about it, getting a secondary message is of prime importance. Unlike teachers, you do not have a choice when it comes to the counselor's letter of recommendation. Your counselor most likely has a caseload of students applying to colleges. Therefore, if you want your counselor to write you a fantastic letter of recommendation, provide your counselor with a brag sheet with all of your accomplishments.

Better yet, make regular visits with your counselor throughout your high school journey so that you are not just another nameless, faceless caseload. If you feel a strong passion for a particular subject, shout it out to your counselor. Describe not only what you have learned and how well you have performed but what contributions you expect to make in the college of your choice and beyond. When your counselor is about to draft your recommendation letter, make sure that you mention your significant challenges and experiences.

Are My Letters Confidential?

Some teachers or faculty will gladly show you their letters of recommendation before they send them. They understand that you might want to verify facts and correct any mistakes. Others are more hidden. It is up to the recommender. Usually, most letters are expected to be confidential. If your teacher does not wholeheartedly volunteer to show you the written recommendation before submission, do not insist that he or she do so. If you do, you are communicating, in so many words, that you do not trust the teacher to write a persuasive letter of recommendation. If you feel hesitant about the teacher's willingness to actively promote you, move on to the next teacher. Remember some will, some won't, who cares! Nowadays, most letters will be submitted by faculty online, so you may miss the opportunity to see a hard copy of them. In rare instances, if your teacher wants to send an old-fashioned hard copy to the college of your choice, provide a pre-stamped and a self pre-addressed envelope.

Your Rights Under FERPA

Though letters of recommendation might be confidential during the submission process, you have a right under Federal law to look at your recommendations after the college files them. Bear in mind that most letters of recommendation include forms with checkboxes. Follow the letter's instructions. Check off if you want to sign away your rights under the FERPA (Family Educational Rights and Privacy Act), although legally speaking, it is generally not a good idea to sign away your privacy rights. However, in this case, you might want to.

Following Up with Recommendation Requests

You must follow up with your recommenders at least one week, preferably two, before your deadlines. As a general principle, you ALWAYS want to follow up with every request, every application submission, or anything that could significantly impact your life. It is your responsibility to ensure that the wheels of the application process are running smoothly and efficiently. Make sure to thank your teacher by writing a handwritten thank-you letter, perhaps even a gift. Gratitude goes a long way.

Letters of recommendation are a significant part of your application. They reveal much to an admission officer about your social skills and other matters not mentioned in your transcript.

Build relationships with your teachers and ask for them early, and you will get a great letter. They will be part of your application discussed in the next chapter.

CHAPTER 9

The Brave New World of College Application Basics

To learn and not to do is really not to learn. To know and not to do is really not to know.
Stephen R. Covey, *The 7 Habits of Highly Effective People.*

It is time to direct all of your knowledge toward an actionable cause. It is time to apply to the college of your choice. We live in the best of times to explore many colleges at once. No longer do you need to slave over a typewriter with a bottle of correction fluid. With the click of a mouse and the push of a few buttons, you can blast your college application to several prospective colleges that might admit you. However, careless mistakes can prevent you from getting selected. Watch out for spelling errors, typos, and other unforgivable grammatical faux pas. Be careful! Review your application carefully. Given your investment of time, you owe it to yourself to apply correctly to get your application right from the very start. To err is human, except when you fill out an application to the college of your choice.

What Happens if You Miss a Deadline?

One of my clients did not get into a select college because she missed a detail in the application and consequently did not submit it on time. However, don't despair if this happens to you. If you miss a deadline, contact the admission office and explain why you missed it. If you missed the deadline because of pure negligence, there is a slim chance opportunity that the admission officers will consider your application.

However, if you missed the deadline due to circumstances beyond your control, here are some helpful hints to reapply:

- Reapply during the following year.
- Apply during the spring when there are fewer students on campus.
- Find out if your college has **rolling admissions**. Schools with rolling admissions do not have deadlines.
- Wait for about one year and take courses at a community college, travel, learn a new language, or pursue a hobby.

Missing a deadline can ultimately cost you because reviewers only screen applications when there are spots left after the regular application cycle. Plus, your application will not receive top priority for housing and financial aid. Avoid this problem, and I highly recommend you do the following:

- Keep a calendar with urgent deadlines. Review it often and check items as you complete them.
- Contact the admission office if you missed the deadline or have any questions concerning the application process.
- Get your application in early. *I cannot emphasize this enough!* Early applications receive top priority for financial aid and housing.

Making a List and Checking it Twice

After combing a catalog of several potential colleges to attend, your objective is to zero in on at least seven excellent schools that catch your eye and your heart. Within this narrow listing, choose some that are highly desired yet very selective. The remainder of schools that are quality institutions, yet realistically attainable, should fall within the odds of fifty-fifty. During the application process, keep an open mind to schools that seem beyond reason to reach, while others should be easy to attain. That way, you are not putting all of your eggs in one basket. However, as mentioned in an earlier chapter, you want to identify your dream school, the one and only, the chosen one, and pursue it with a burning desire, focus, and faith. Apply often apply early and discretely. Keep your open, but never settle for less than the best. W. Clement Stone once said, "Aim for the moon. If you miss, you may hit a star" (BrainyQuote).

Online Application Options

The online application process is like floating on a cloud on a sunny day. You can instantaneously blast several applications to select schools and receive instant confirmation. Not only that, what you submit on your computer is what the admissions officers see on their end. The most prodigious online platform is the **Common Application** (www.commonapp.org). As of this writing, you can apply to more than 800 colleges with only one application. Amazing! You are no longer limited to geography in your quest for the right college. The Common Application is an efficient system that connects you to schools all around the world. You no longer need to enter your information details to every single college. One application does it all. However, some colleges have adopted the Common Application in place of their own. Others have kept their platform. Bear in mind that many universities require you to self-report your grades during the application time, instead of requiring a school to submit a transcript. Make sure that you thoroughly understand the nuances of grade reporting, typical application submission, and how each school goes about it.

The Advantages and Disadvantages of Applying Early

There are two strategies to apply early: **Early Decision**

(ED) and Early Action (EA). These plans are excellent for students who thoughtfully reviewed their college plans. However, there are some limitations. About 450 colleges use early decision or early action plans. A few colleges are offering a noncommittal choice called **single-choice early action.** Under this plan, students cannot apply ED or EA at other colleges. For more information, visit the College Board (https://professionals.collegeboard.org/guidance/applications/early).

Early Decision

An **Early Decision (ED)** is *permanent.* Accepted students as an ED application must attend. For more information about the early decision or early action, visit the College Board at (https://professionals.collegeboard.org/guidance/applications/early).

Early Decision Musts
- Apply early (usually in November) to your select college
- Receive admission from college much sooner than the standard admission date (typically before December)
- May apply to other colleges
- Agree to only one college under early decision with financial aid sufficient for the family
- Withdraw other applications if ED accepts you

- Mail a nonrefundable deposit well before May 1st.

In 2016, a unique online application platform took the college admissions world by storm called the **Coalition for Access Affordability and Success** (www.coalitionforcollegeaccess.org). More than 140 leading institutions, select colleges and universities embraced this platform. The mission is to offer diverse students, especially those who are of lower-income and under-represented, with student aid and other resources to help them succeed in college. The coalition platform has essential resources. Students can store their application documents in a virtual locker and invite counselors, mentors, and other concerned parties to help them make college happen. Applying to 100 colleges is easy. Colleges vigilantly screen applicants to ensure they sincerely desire to apply to their hallowed institution. To ensure that your select school notices you do the following:

Visit the campus if you did not schedule a guided tour, make an appointment with the admissions office to gain visibility and personalized attention and answers to any of your questions:

- Attend the college fair in your area and speak with representatives.
- Identify your number one dream school as your top priority among the many schools you plan to submit your application.
- Make sure that you read directions and fully complete

the college writing supplement, noting the exact word count of the essay.

Although the college application seems tedious, there are many online tools and resources to make the process run smoother and more organized than ever before. Still, it is crucial to begin the application process early because deadlines approach quickly. PROOFREAD YOUR APPLICATION. Make a list of all your target schools and their websites, keep copies of everything. Most importantly, follow up with admissions several days after you submit your application. Never assume that your select college received all of your materials. The burden of a submission rests squarely on your shoulders. Now that you have the basics of the application process under your belt, it is time for you to learn how to craft the essay of champions for you to shine as an applicant.

CHAPTER 10

Writing the Essay of Champions

Your visions will become clear only when you can look into your own heart. Who looks outside, dreams; who looks inside, awakes.
C.G. Jung.

For students who have not taken writing-intensive courses in high school or college, crafting a well-articulated admissions essay may feel like walking along the edge of a cliff blindfolded. Perhaps they received harsh criticism from teachers and peers or misguided commentary from loved ones who told them that language mastery is not their strong suit. They may believe that whatever they write will never be right because grading is subjective. They affirm that their humble essay will not stand out with admissions officers because the competition to get into their dream school is fierce. Is this you? Do you believe you're not good enough, smart enough, or articulate enough to craft an essay?

It is possible to win the approval of evaluators by understanding how admission officials will evaluate your essay.

If you did well in school and identified your mission and vision for college admission, your shot at winning the approval of admissions officers is strong. Are you still doubtful? Read on!

Know the Mission and Vision of Your College

I can't emphasize enough how important it is to know the mission of your selected school. In chapter 1, I mention the importance of knowing *your* mission and vision to clarify your values, to identify your reasons for going to college. Also, it is essential to identify the mission or purpose of your selected school. I once worked with a student who felt passionate about attending an excellent school. However, he felt stuck. He felt intimidated because he believed that his dream school had all the power, and he had none as an applicant. I have mentioned this a few times in this book, but I will mention it again: *The college admission process is not a one-way street.* You are checking out the college to make sure that it is the right college for you. At the same time, the admission officers at your chosen school are checking you out. By knowing the mission of the school, you see the school's values and what direction you need to take to make the most favorable impression.

Why the Essay is Important

The essay is an opportunity for officers to subjectively learn more about your dreams, goals, values, communication skills, and how you package yourself on paper. It is also an excellent way for you to communicate a strength or quality that grades and standardized test scores cannot reveal. It enables admissions officers an opportunity to take a second look at a candidate, in case an application looks questionable.

Who Will Read Your Essay?

A committee of admission officers who will evaluate your essay tends to be young, friendly, and outgoing as opposed to the stiff-necked, stuffy-shirts. Most of them enjoy working with students. They typically remain employed for about three years.

Volunteer Work and Internships

Do not merely state a volunteer position or internship. Describe precisely what volunteer activities you did, what you have learned, and how you grew. If you volunteered for instance, what did you learn? How did the people you meet affect you? How did you impact them? How did your position influence your education? How did it help you in your career decision?

How Will You Contribute to the College of Your Choice?

What sets you apart from other applicants? What are your unique skills?

Many bright, conscientious, committed students

sleepwalk their way through the college application essay. They are so focused on preparing for exams to get into the top-notch Ivy League schools that they forget that part of the application process is their self-disclosed. Many students do not realize that the college admission essay is a unique opportunity to display your uniqueness compared to other highly qualified students. It is a way to show how you are more than your grades and your test scores. They feel intimidated by their perceived inability to express themselves on paper or recall their grammar lessons from the seventh grade. The key to overcoming essay shyness is preparedness. Understand the kinds of questions asked. Practice answering them until you know them as well as you know your first name. If you do all these things, you will write the essay of champions.

Typical Essay Questions:

Tell Me About Yourself

In what ways have you grown intellectually? Since test scores recommendations and grades reveal so little about a student, what can you say about yourself that obvious on a college application? What's great about this kind of question is that it addresses a topic in which you are an expert: yourself. You can discuss where you went to school, what you learned, and the unique experiences that make you a must-admit in the college of your dreams.

Why Us?

Like the creative essay about you, the "us" essay is a perfect opportunity for you to speak about yourself. You can discuss your academic and vocational interests, and why you are choosing college X over college Y. You have already investigated many schools. You read about them; you itemized them, visited them, and discovered how you feel about them at the heart level. You hopefully have interviewed several faculties, especially professors, and made some stable connections who may vouch for you as a promising student. Most importantly, you have identified your mission and the mission of your selected college and determined how you and your choice college are a match made in heaven.

However, you must know where you are going and why. Review the college catalog and any relevant information about your college of choice to highlight attributes about that college that appeal to you. Keep in mind that colleges are ultimately interested in intelligent, curious, stable students attuned to their mission and who are self-aware.

Tell Us About a Challenge

Be very careful when answering this kind of question. Colleges are looking for a thoughtful, focused student aware of his/her limitations, strengths, and how they will contribute to your college success. They want to know how well you will handle challenges and how well you stand up to challenges when life knocks you down. Your essay is not a confessional. You want to present yourself at your best. You want to show the admission officers why you are the best candidate for your college of choice.

One of my clients almost sent an essay in which she stated that she failed courses because she did not take school seriously. If she had submitted this essay through the common application, many colleges would have rejected her. It is okay to admit failure, but you want to show how you have grown from your mistakes and how they have made you a better person. Keep in mind those admission officers who are reading your essays are real human beings—just like you and me! They perceive you as a whole person, not merely a set of grades and test scores. Be that as it may, you want to adequately describe a personal or academic challenge that puts you in a positive light.

First of all, be transparent and forthcoming. Do not downplay or try to avoid addressing your mistakes altogether. Otherwise, the admission committee may feel that you are avoiding responsibility and will not be impressed with your story. Instead, admit what happened and emphasize what you have learned and how you have grown.

Also, bear in mind that you do not necessarily need a 4.0 to get into many colleges. While grades are significant, they are not always necessary to get into outstanding schools. Describing how you persevered and overcame hardship may convince the admission officers that you are a strong candidate. In your essay, mention additional stressors that kept you from performing at your best. Did you suffer from an illness? Did you endure hardships at home? How did they impact you? What did you learn from these challenges? How you address obstacles that affected your performance will determine how the admission committee will consider you as a candidate.

The Creative Question

The original question is an opportunity for you to take a contrived problem, look past the guidelines, and use your imagination to write engaging stories with compelling descriptions.

Here are some types of questions you might be asked to test your creative process:

- Describe a mentor or teacher who had a significant impact on your personal and intellectual growth.
- Of all the books you have read, which one's have had the most significant effect on you, and why? Ask and answer the most crucial question that you wish we would have asked.
- Explain why a particular day in the recent past continues to be relevant to you.

Keep in mind that the creative essay is all about you, but with a wrinkle. While you have much liberty on creatively connecting with prominent or historical figures from the past, do not feel tempted to write an essay with no substance. Pay close attention to details about national issues and verify for accuracy. Though it is hard to stay informed, write an informed paper.

Additionally, every essay must have a purpose. Just because an essay topic is creative does not mean that you have a license to go crazy and wander astray. However, admissions personnel enjoy a little quirkiness in an essay as long as it's grounded with factual information, framed around a cohesive, well-written paper with a purpose. Remember the golden rules of essay writing.

The One-Paragraph Essay

Winston Churchill once said, "If I had more time, I would have written a shorter letter." In the spirit of Churchill, some colleges test the ability of prospective students to think on their feet and write the contents of a full essay in only one paragraph. This particular kind of essay is challenging because it requires one to synthesize and prioritize essential points. One way to tackle this kind of essay is to write about 500 words and then edit it down to around 100. As you trim the verbiage, find out if you could say the same idea with fewer words.

Submit Academic Writing

If some colleges require you to submit a sample essay, it's okay to send a high school essay. Most college and high school essays are similar. However, you do not want to turn in a massive term paper or one that is not academic. The best writing to turn in is one that is short, well-written, and illuminating on a history topic, a creative short piece. Make sure that the copy you send is legible and soft on the eyes.

Although there are no terrible topics or beginnings, there are a few things you should keep in mind when writing. You want to make your first impression a lasting good impression. Your opening sentence should be engaging, thought-provoking, and essentially summarize the main ideas of your essay. When generating the essay, it is best to talk it out or brainstorm with friends, parents, tutors, or someone capable of giving you supportive, but constructive feedback. Be forthcoming and genuine about your topic. Don't write to please the admissions personnel. If you write an intelligent, thought-provoking response, you will make a positive impression.

Avoid Overused Clichés

Do not overuse clichés. Certain expressions like, "A bird in the hand is worth two in the bush" or "all for one, and one for all" may seem like normal, acceptable speech, but these expressions are overused. Colleges appreciate articulate students with an excellent command of English. Don't spoil your paper by loading it with stale, overused clichés.

In addition to clichés, do not over quote. To sound well informed, many students flood their essay with quotes, yet they never explain these quotes. Use them sparingly. An essay tests your ability to reply to a topic with creative, analytical skills thoughtfully.

Avoid These Practices

Do not write an essay that someone else has submitted

Keep in mind that your objective is to demonstrate your uniqueness. Write your essay as if you were talking directly to a teacher or an admission committee. You can ask someone to edit your essay later. But don't—and *I repeat*—don't make someone else write your essay! During an interview, the admission board wants to know that how you represent yourself on paper matches how you come across in person. If the admission board discovers that you did not write the essay, your chances of admission are slim!

Do Not Worry About Writing the Perfect Essay

If, for example, you are asked to write about a world topic, your goal isn't to say everything that could ever be said. Instead, you will want to share your beliefs and interpretation of critical facts.

Write Engaging, Intelligent Essays

Admissions officers and college professors admire students who enjoy engaging in intelligent, reasonable, and civil debates. They appreciate those who embrace diversity while retaining their individuality. You do not need to write the perfect essay.

Watch Out for the Shorter Essays

Ensure that your essay is the exact number of words that are requested. Make every word count. Whenever you answer a question, always explain why. If you are asked to describe how you demonstrated leadership, and why it is significant. For example, one of my students founded and directed a medical club at his high school. During the summer, he volunteered as a nursing assistant at a low-income hospital in a third-world country. He spent months assisting children who had leukemia. After discovering that the hospital did not have air-conditioning, he raised money through his medical club to buy an air conditioner. He accomplished this amazing feat because he was focused, determined, and knew how to bring people together to support a cause. As a result of his efforts, he brought some comfort and joy to many children suffering from unspeakable pain.

Grammar Considerations

Make sure you brush up on the basic grammar rules or learn them and know them. The purpose of grammar is not merely to identify errors and correctness in sentences; it helps everyone communicate sentences and paragraphs in a clear, engaging, understandable manner. The following guidelines should help to ensure you effectively use grammar to convey your ideas in an essay.

Transitions

Writing transitions is the art of shifting from one idea to the next without jolting your reader. An ideal essay is a series of thoughts, strung together in well-articulated paragraphs with transitional phrases that link them together. Some transitions compare and contrast, display time sequences, and so on. For a complete list of transitions and how to use them, check out: https://writingcenter.unc.edu/tips-and-tools/transitions/.

Write in the Active Voice

With an active voice, the subject does the action designated by a verb. In a passive voice, the subject is receiving the action. Here are examples of using the active and the passive voice:

Active voice: Melissa cooked dinner.
Passive voice: the dinner was cooked by Melissa.

Show, Don't Tell

Make your essay come alive by helping admission officers see what you see, hear what you hear, taste what you taste, and feel what you feel. Instead of saying, "I went swimming," say this: "I dove into a warm swimming pool in my backyard and enjoyed the warm sensation of the water against my bare skin."

Steps to Writing the Essay

1. Brainstorm.

2. Write everything related to your topic freely and spontaneously.
3. Read directions carefully.
4. Write the essay.
5. Do not copy someone else's essay.
6. Take a break for a few days. After you write your essay, pause. It is challenging to write a quality essay when you are too attached to it. By taking a break, you can look at your essay with fresh eyes.
7. Proofread your essay with spell checker and grammar check, there is no reason to submit a manuscript littered with careless errors.
8. Do not procrastinate. Write the essay immediately. Do not wait until the last minute. Deadlines approach quickly.

Ultimately, with writing an essay, keep in mind that you are the author. You are the one applying to a particular college that you've methodically researched and visited. You have unique perspectives and experiences that cannot be matched by anyone else. Also, bear in mind that the essay, or personal statement, is only one criterion for college admission.

The purpose of the college essay is to show the admissions department why you are a good match for your select school. While grades and test scores are essential, they do not paint a complete picture of the ideal student. Ultimately, humans will be attending the school—not grades and test scores. In your essay, you can demonstrate your creativity, your determination, your values, and how you can contribute significantly to your school and your community. With practice and mastery of grammar and writing skills, you can write the essay of champions! Writing a compelling essay will not only help you get into college, but it can also help you with obtaining financial aid, discussed in the next chapter.

CHAPTER 11

The Rudiments of Financial Aid

Education costs money, but then so does ignorance.
Sir C. Moser.

Though financial aid is not one of the more favorable aspects of the college admission process, it is essential. However, the college admission game is mostly about financing your education. If you have any doubts about the importance of financial aid, consider this article by *Forbes* (Onink). "College Costs Could Total as Much as $334,000 in Four Years."

- The cost of attending a private Ivy League college for four years is roughly $68,000.
- A four-year public college is over $28,000 per year.

In a CNBC.com article, "Here's how much more expensive it is for you to go to college than it was for your parents, the cost of tuition has increased by 213%" (Martin).

Unless you are Bill Gates, take heed for mastering financial aid basics as this may be your only saving grace to afford college. Even though many schools are less likely to provide much financial aid, they are willing to offer significant discounts based on need and merit. Some schools have also lightened a load of tuition costs by eliminating debt, even for those with families who earn above $150,000 per year.

Understanding the basics of financial aid will enable you to fund your dream school. Many people do not apply to outstanding schools because they think that they cannot afford them. Think that the cost of attending "Working closely with admissions, I noticed that colleges might offer discount rates that might be as much as 40-50% or more discounted. By understanding the financial aid process, you can find significant savings. At the same time, I come from the belief that a student should focus on the institution, not the cost of that institution. If you do find the right connections, you will get the training you need to obtain a career that excites you. The most important thing is that the college must be the right fit or the student. That is why it is essential to take many college tours, explore the campus, and make sure that it is the right fit" (Bayer). The right connections, information and mindset, and understanding of financial aid will place you in the best position to land in your dream school and your chosen field.

The Fundamentals of Financial Aid

College administered financial aid is either academic merit or need-based:

- Private institutions are the best places to consider financial aid based on need. Consulting with parents about how much they could contribute toward tuition would be a wise course of action.
- Budget the costs of room, board, transportation, travel books, and supplies. Calculating the amount of awarded aid is determined by the Expected Family Contribution (EFC), the amount that the college determines that a family can afford. College administered financial aid is either academic merit or need-based.
- Private institutions are the best places to consider financial aid based on need. Consulting with parents about how much they could contribute toward tuition would be a wise course of action.

Family Outing at the Financial Aid Office

Make sure that you and your family visit the financial aid office. If your family has unforeseen medical costs, a variable income, or anything out of the ordinary, visiting the financial aid office may offer solutions or options. Check out a net price calculator to determine what your actual costs for you and your family might be with your circumstances. You can find one by visiting the College Board website at www.collegeboard.org. Colleges use an index number to determine your eligibility to receive financial aid. If the colleges determine that your **EFC (Expected Family Contribution)** is more than $60,000 explore merit-based scholarships to offset the cost. If your EFC is less than $20,000, check out schools committed to providing need-based aid. Meanwhile, it is essential to distinguish the difference between merit and need-based scholarships.

Need-Based Aid Versus Merit-Based Aid

According to an article in the Princeton Review, a mediocre or high-achieving student has the same chances of eligibility for the highest amount of federal aid. Students will be awarded either on need or academic merit.

Merit-Based Aid

One can receive a **Merit Scholarship** based on academic, artistic, or athletic merit. In this competitive, frenzy of academic prestige, colleges have conjured a magic formula to earn money by giving it away. Their strategy is to give it away to students who are performing at the highest academic level and who can also pay most of the bill. The more money that a college invests in merit-based awards, the less it has to give away to those who need it most. The bottom line is that if you are an outstanding student, your good grades will pay off in dollars as well as invisibility to select schools that want you. Very few prestigious schools offer aid based solely on a needed basis. The less prestigious institutions rely on merit- based assistance to improve their rankings. Keep in mind that even though a merit scholarship. In *Paying for College without Going Broke,* Kalman Chany exhaustively guides parents on how to leverage their income and assets to qualify for as much aid as possible.

What are Need-Based Aid Scholarships?

Need-based scholarships do not discriminate by any means apart from financial aid. Considering the assets and income of the prospective student and his or her family needs are essential considerations. Academic performance and athletic ability have no bearing on need-based aid.

Determining Student Financial Needs

- Fill out the **Free Application for Federal Student Aid (FAFSA).** The FAFSA will ask questions about family income and assets then compute the need from a mathematical formula that sends the information to the select colleges.
- It is essential to complete the FAFSA as soon as possible. Eligibility for Grants depends upon a first-come-first-serve basis. Even if you must guess, it is

better to file directly.

Pell Grant
- Students automatically qualify for a pool of and loans are higher for those who do not receive Pell.
- More than 60% of Pell Grant recipients student loans to complete college.

FAFSA (Free Application for Federal Student Aid)
(http://fafsa.ed.gov) determines the following:
- Income
- Assets
- Parents income and assets, if you are a dependent (students receive Pell grants)
- Family household size
- Number of family members
- Number of members attending college (excluding parents)

Where to obtain more knowledge about Financial Aid

- www.finaid.org

The FinAid site offers detailed coverage of every nuance of financial aid.

- www.fastweb.com

    The most in-depth and comprehensive listing of scholarships on the Internet.

- www.fafsa.gov

    This site is the hub of financial assistance for the Federal government, especially the Free Application for Federal Student Aid. All applicants must complete and submit their FAFSA online.

Demystifying financial aid is crucial in the college admission process because college is a significant investment. Before you enroll or apply for any additional funding sources, you will need to fill out the FAFSA (Free Application for Federal Student Aid). Understand the costs of grants, scholarships, and loans. For the majority of students, the primary source of financial aid will be need-based aid. Regardless of your economic situation, you will discover a wide range of opportunities to lessen the financial burden. As you will see in the next chapter, there are many different scholarships and other sources of money you might obtain.

CHAPTER 12

Finding the Money so That Money Finds You the College of Your Choice

Show me the money.
Jerry Maguire.

Scholarships are an essential but often overlooked part of the financial aid package. Along with federal aid discussed in chapter 11, you should explore a wide range of scholarship possibilities at your school or through private sources. Don't feel for one split second that you might not qualify for a scholarship because you are either too rich or too poor. Don't overlook seeking scholarships because you think you are not academically accomplished or popular. Keep in mind that financing is a critical part of your college education for EVERYONE. Despite preconceived notions you may have about receiving free money, do not leave any stone unturned. Apply early and apply often.

Many feel hesitant to apply for scholarships because they think that they do not deserve to receive money, "they didn't pay for." If you entertain these thoughts for even a millisecond, I want you to dismiss them right now! When the government, companies, or private individuals provide you with a scholarship, they are not giving money away for free. Technically, they are loaning you their money. They are banking on the possibility that you will do well and contribute to society. By accepting any scholarship money, you necessarily agree to a contract between you and the donor that you will use college as a means to demonstrate your power beyond measure to lighten the world, like a supernova with your gifts. Trust me; you are worth it! Don't shut out scholarships out of fear. You need them! You deserve them! Do you still feel doubtful? Read on!

More than 100,000 seniors did not apply for Pell Grants (www.scholarshippoints.com). As a result, they missed out on more than $396,401,205 in potential federal grant aid. Do not let this happen to you. Some students have found so much money; they did not need to work during the academic year. Go to https://scholarships.com and conduct a thorough search for available scholarships. Also, go to the financial aid office at the college of your choice and apply for whatever scholarships are available. Get as much information from as many sources as possible. The more information you have, the better equipped you will be to receive supplemental scholarships to complement your financial aid package.

Important Steps to Finding a Scholarship

- Read directions. Pay close attention to details, especially deadlines.
- Read the fine print.
- Everyone can qualify for a scholarships.
- Play to your strengths by conducting a free scholarship search. You can find a plethora of them from scholarships.com or from a wide range of online sources.

Making the Grade

According to Steven Robello, an educational consultant for the Pacific Rim College Planning in Honolulu, Hawaii scholarship says that worlds open for students who maintain a 3.6 GPA or higher. Do well in school. Make the grade. Many students who come from families without a college background do not know how to help their children. Therefore, it is helpful to obtain a mentor to help with everything necessary to get high grades (Robello).

Write an Amazing Essay

Although I thoroughly explained how to write winning essays in chapter 10, I am reviewing some of the same techniques in this chapter because essay writing is a vital skill that you need to get into the college of your dreams and beyond.

Burn my advice in your brain until you know them cold! You will be happy that you did. Keep the following points in mind:

- Many hours and countless amounts of energy are needed to write a stellar essay to win scholarship money.
- Most scholarship reviewers of the essays have specifics about the length and word count. If you ignore the requirements, scholarship donors will not consider you. You do not need to be an outstanding writer to receive a fantastic scholarship package if you follow directions to the letter.
- Answer each part of the essay question with general statements supported by examples, evidence, anecdotes, and whatever additional information you can gather to address the problem.
- Many essay questions do not require a thesis, but the essay questions which ask about your leadership abilities or a personal challenge that you have overcome like you to speak from the heart.

How to Write an Engaging Essay

1. **Know your audience.** Who is offering the scholarship money? What organization does the scholarship represent? Are you asked to express personal hardship? Is there a character quality or a community service

that could be in line with the donor? Regardless of what kind of question is presented to you, the effectiveness of your reply depends on the degree of thorough research you have conducted. If you have done your homework, you will be head and shoulders above the other applicants who cut and paste and slap generic, canned answers on a page.

2. **Plan as early as possible.** The more time you allow for pondering the questions of the scholarship donor, the better you will be able to write a concise, targeted response.

3. **Craft personal, passionate, and vivid sentences.** Remember that good writing is showing, not telling. For example, do not just mention that you like teaching or studying biology. Mention how your struggles with joint pain inspired you to study chiropractic medicine. Do not merely say you like environmental sciences. Describe how an injury, due to a chemical spill, inflamed you to learn about eco-friendly cleaning and how you felt inspired to motivate others to promote safer measures for the planet. Placing your heart, soul, and unique interests and life journey in a memorable essay will draw positive attention from a would-be scholarship donor. Let your humanity shine on paper.

4. **Proof your work.** Find a professional editor, an educational coach, or a friend to review your essay with an editor's eye. An error-free paper can make a huge difference. If you are unable to find anyone to critique your work, do it yourself objectively. Read your essay aloud. Pretend that you are saying it to a close friend. If any part of your article sounds choppy or disjointed, fix it. Watch for grammatical and spelling errors. If you planned well in advance, which you should, then you will have plenty of time to cast your essay aside for a few days and re-read it with a fresh objective eye.

By knowing your audience, planning your essay well in advance, crafting sentences with pizzazz, and proofing your work, you will be amazed by the different amounts of scholarships that could be yours. Show your due diligence, and donors will show you the money.

Six Great Sites to Look for Scholarships

Fastweb
www.Fastweb

The leading online resource in finding a scholarship is your one-stop, go-to source for all of your scholarship needs.

Scholarship Points

www.Scholarshippoints.com

Created in 2006, The Scholarship Points program helps students qualify for dozens of scholarships without the hassle of filling out applications and writing essays. The ScholarshipPoints.com community enables high school and college students to be eligible to earn points and enter scholarship activities.

Cappex

www.cappex.com

If you are looking to get admission and deadlines on several campuses at once, Cappex is your college decision headquarters. You can access more than 1.4 million student reviews and tag colleges that want students with your interests.

Scholarship

www.scholarship

Whether you are a high school student, college student, nontraditional adult learner, you can complete a profile to match you with scholarships, grants for universities, organizations, foundations, government, and more.

College Board

www.collegeboard.org

A non-profit organization that develops and administers standardized tests promotes college readiness and provides a plethora of information on scholarships including tools and resources in the area of college planning.

College Net

www.collegenet.com

With CollegeNet, you earn money by writing about topics that persuade others to vote on you. Through the voting process, you can exercise control over the judgment. If you are not a college student and you have no student loan, you cannot win a scholarship.

Though the almighty American dollar has devalued and inflation has risen along with college tuition, you can qualify for some financial aid and a plethora of scholarships for admission if you know where to look and how to prepare for essays that shine with personality. The choice is yours. The money is out there. Get it! In the next chapter, you will learn about other financial strategies to leverage the college of your choice.

CHAPTER 13

The Right Major at the Right College at the Right Time

Planning is bringing the future into the present so that you can do something about it now.
Alan Lakein.

Since many believe they cannot send their children to the college of their choice, they tearfully and fearfully apply to any college they can, hoping that any one of them will accept them. What they do not realize about financial aid, according to Ed Smelich, a certified college planning specialist, is that "it does not necessarily go to those who need it the most but often goes to those who understand it the most" (Smelich). Still, many put off planning for college, hoping that college will happen, braced for their potential let down. For that reason, the late stage of college planning has begun. However, when most people hear about someone planning for college, they think, "Oh, you just had a baby, buy a UGMA (Uniform Gift to Minors Account) or a 529 Plan." A **529 Plan** is a tax-advantaged investment vehicle in the United States that encourages saving money for higher education in the future. It is a special savings plan. Each 529 has an account owner who maintains the investments and selects a beneficiary. The account holder and the beneficiary may be the same individual. There are many plans available and you are not limited merely to your state's plan. For more information about 529 plans, visit https://www.savingforcollege.com/intro-to-529s/what-is-a-529-plan. A **UGMA** is an act in some states that allows minors to own assets, including securities (Traded certificates with monetary value). You can establish a UGMA account on behalf of a child without the need for an attorney to create a special trust fund (assets developed by a grantor to provide financial security to a minor, most often a child or a grandchild). For more information about UGMAs, visit https://www.thebalance.com/beginners-guide-to-ugma-and-utma-custodial-accounts-4060475.

  The problem is that most people are not thinking about long-term savings and investment plans for college. They are caught up with paying the mortgage and burdened with the costs of raising a child. Saving for college or just saving period is a luxury. Furthermore, those very savings plans will decrease the amount of potential financial aid. To add insult to injury, many families do not even carry life insurance to protect themselves in case of a catastrophic event.

According to Hermie Bachus, an agent at an insurance company called PFA, more than 100,000,000 people in America are underinsured. Furthermore, Hermie says that with the existing savings plans for college, such as the 529 savings plans, parents will not be able to save much money by the time their child turns 18. Hermie also says that our education system should start teaching students about how to invest and save their money for college long before they apply. When it is near time for their kids to go to college, most parents will want to do just about anything to send them to college and get them into the college of their choice. Sadly, they will pay the sticker price of a selected college without question (Bachus). The good news is that there are strategies for students and families to manipulate their EFC (Expected Family Contribution). When students apply for their FAFSA (Free Application for Federal Student Aid), they can receive the maximum aid instead of paying the sticker price for tuition. It is the form that families fill out to apply for federal grants, loans and work-study, and what are necessarily tuition discounts, funds for college students. It is administered by the US Department of Education, which provides around $150 billion in student aid each year. The EFC is a term for the college financial aid process in the United States to determine an applicant's eligibility for need-based federal student aid and, in many cases, state and institutional college aid. Most applicants believe that the tuition for the college of their choice and their EFC cannot be changed. If they see an outstanding, prestigious college priced at 65k per year, their knee-jerk response is to say, "next" and then move on. However, with a little research, understanding of the financial aid process, and the willingness to challenge the price tag of a selected college, an applicant can pay considerably less for college admission.

The out-of-pocket costs can differ significantly compared to the quoted cost of attendance or sticker price. For instance, when buying a car today, many would never dream of paying the sticker price for a vehicle. In the 1970s, however, people did not question the price of a car. If they wanted an orange Datsun 240Z, they would say, "I want that orange car!" They did not care about the cost of the car because the car was in such high demand that there was no negotiation, and therefore, no other choice other than to pay full sticker price. They were ready to buy the car on the spot and did not realize that negotiation was an option. Today, people are a lot smarter about car buying. With college, however, most do not imagine that they have any negotiating options. However, if an institution has any empty seats, that institution may look at other factors besides the cost of the college.

Since many college applicants do not realize that they have some say about the final cost of their tuition, they will pay whatever the college tells them to pay. No questions asked. At the same time, they hope and pray that the Federal Government, and the college itself, will offset some of their costs with grants, loans, or work-study. They hope for the best and believe that there are only specific colleges they can choose because of the limited amount of money they hope that they can get. With proactive research and a college planning advisor, it is possible to expand your selection of college choices. The scope of this chapter is to shed light on some resources to help students get into the best college for them instead of limiting their choices solely based on money. While many books on college focus exclusively on the general logistics of getting into college, the purpose of this book is to find the *best* college for you, the student, and the families funding the college and determine if the best college is in a rural area or the heart of a major city.

Is it a big school, a small school, or a party school or pure academic school? Is there a lot of diversity? Many choose a school either for its reputation or purely personal reasons such as liking the school because it has a great football program or because that is where their boyfriend/girlfriend is going.

Rather than choosing a school because of a great football program or because that is where a boyfriend/girlfriend is going, families and individuals should ask themselves what the best-fit college for the student is. Some of those parameters might include a large school vs. small school, party vs. academic, rural vs. urban, close to home vs. another side of the country.

Students must make sure that they are academically suited at their selected college and do well on the SAT or ACT and getting good grades. GPA is enormous, and many colleges are taking a close look at high school ranking. Then they need to be sure of their intended major based on interests and aptitudes derived from a career assessment or personality profile. But how realistic is it for a teenager to know what their career path will be? Except for a few who have their career path practically from birth, most teenagers are unclear about how to plan for college. Therefore, I highly recommend that parents set their children up with a professional college planning expert to help them with the right assessments to target the right colleges, with the right major and at the right price.

In addition to prepping for colleges, career assessment is critical to ensure that students are choosing the best program that will not only bring them fulfillment but save them a tremendous amount of money in the long run. On average, 80 percent of students change their majors. Additionally, the average student changes their major three times. At some point during their college journey, a college that was four years is now 5.6 years. A big-ticket Ivy League college that initially cost $65,000 is now $100,000 more just because you are going to be there for 1.6 years longer.

Once a student prepares for standardized testing, achieves excellent grades, and sets up a career program, the next step to getting into the college of their choice is to fill out their FAFSA application correctly. This process helps get them the maximum aid by utilizing legal strategies to shelter assets that would typically be visible to the formula for a family's EFC (Expected Family Contribution) and make them invisible so that the method does not see them. If, for example, a family has $200,000 in their checking account, their assessed EFC is at 5.65% of any amount more significant than the family's asset protection allowance. Since this particular family seems to have substantial assets and earn an income of around $200,000, the government may wonder why this family needs help in the first place. As far as the government and the college institution are concerned, this family should be able to write a check for the entire amount of tuition.

The cash value of a life insurance policy is the cash amount offered to a system owned by the issuing life carrier upon the cancelation of the contract. Exploring the possibilities of cash-value life insurance policy is essential for many reasons. In particular, if the unthinkable happens and the mother or father passes away, the death benefits will cover the cost of the college, while at the same time help the family receive more financial aid due to the reduction of the EFC. People do not like having inaccessible funds, especially with penalties and converting capital gains to ordinary income. However, this strategy can turn out to be a win-win situation for everyone. The schools are happy because they are filling up seats with quality students that might have otherwise been empty. The parents are so glad they can pay for high-quality education for their children without needing to catastrophically threaten their retirement when it should be growing the most or tap out their home equity and hard-earned savings. It all comes down to education. With a little "outside the box" thinking, it is possible to make private institutions a comparable price to the local state school. Parents need to do their homework by helping their children find best-fit schools for their children. At the same time, they need to position their assets and income to make sure they are funding that school at the most affordable price.

Keep in mind that the school's job, more precisely the financial aid officer's job, is to fill in the empty seats of the college while charging enough money for the school and making the school seem like a desirable choice. If they make it too expensive and do not provide any aid, they will have empty seats. Consequently, no one is going to want to go to that school. With a little planning, the cost of a particular Ivy League college can be reduced down to the same price of the local state school someone ultimately attended. However, before abandoning the possibility of attending a top-quality school just because of money, it is critical to know a school and what kind of aid they give. If you understand the calculation of the aid money of a particular school, the price of a school of ivy league quality can be comparable in price to a state school. How is this possible?

Some elite private colleges may take this financial need number and meet 80-100% of the business need. Some of these needs met will come in the form of gift aid or merit aid, which is free money. The other type of assistance is called self-help or work-study, known as "a loan and a job." There are numerous loan packages, and the school can also offer "work-study" which could be a campus job where the income offsets tuition. Also, some private colleges meet 90% of the financial need in the form of grant aid. Please don't blindly get suckered into paying the sticker price of a high-cost school or abandoning the enrollment at an excellent school just because of money. With a little knowledge of how a school works, the cost of your most prestigious and best-fit college may be plausible.

It is about your willingness to shift perspective and negotiate something to offer the college in exchange for receiving lower tuition. Schools are always looking out for top athletes, gifted students with exceptional talents, diverse heritages, etc. A qualified agent who specializes in college planning can load software and produce demographics of each school so a student with a unique racial and cultural background can target specific schools.

Although there are great resources to help people get into the right college, just as there is a *Buying a Car for Dummies* series of books somewhere out there in the universe, there are similar ones for funding college. Still, not many will run out and buy these books. They are overwhelmed with work, maintaining their household and feeling in desperate need of a quick answer to funding their children's education dozens or hundreds of hours researching all the different ways he can save a few dollars for his child's education. Likewise, a blue-collar worker who has been sweating all day at work is not going to want to invest hours and hours of his time finding ways to send his child to college. For that reason, meeting with a professional who could instantly provide the demographics, the strategies, and the tools to save money on the fly is the best way to go. Clients need to know that the college funding professional is competent and wants to put more money in the hands of the client. Call it a win, win.

Regardless of what path you take to get the best price for the college of your choice, there are some key things that you must do. Never be afraid to negotiate. Remember that the only two things that are certain in this life are death and taxes. Everything else is subjective to some degree and negotiable. Even taxes are negotiable if we legally manipulate them.

Similarly, it is possible to manipulate the EFC. You will never know what you can get until you get the courage to ask for what you need, especially with a college education; it is not set in stone as people traditionally believe it is.

In this situation, a family can reposition assets. Using an **IUL (Index Universal Life)** or other cash-value life insurance policy is a possible solution. An IUL is a policy that offers permanent death benefit protection with cash value for growth. Cash accumulation receives credit based on an index. If the index goes up, you receive interest. If it goes down, you do not. Exploring the possibilities of a cash-value life insurance policy is essential for many reasons. In particular, if the unthinkable happens and the mother or father passes away, the death benefits will cover the cost of the college, while at the same time help the family receive more financial aid due to the reduction of the EFC. People do not like having inaccessible funds, especially with penalties and converting capital gains to ordinary income. However, this strategy can turn out to be a win-win situation for everyone. The schools are happy because they are filling up seats with quality students that might have otherwise been empty. The parents are so glad because they can pay for high-quality education for their children without needing to catastrophically threaten their retirement when it should be growing the most or tap out their home equity and hard-earned savings. It all comes down to education. With a little "outside the box" thinking, it is possible to make private institutions a comparable price to the local state school. Parents need to do their homework to find help their children find the best schools and reposition assets and income to ensure that they obtain the college of choice at the most affordable price.

Keep in mind that no matter how many wrought-iron gates Ivy League colleges place around their hallowed institutions in the form of high tuition costs and tuition standards, they eagerly want students to fill their empty seats. Of course, they do not wish for you, the consumer, to know this. They want you to believe that they are fiercely competitive, and that is how they justify their high sticker price. Keep in mind that you can look at the college admission through the eyes of the admission committee. The quick and convenient way to raise the standards of a college is not necessarily by hiring the best professors, improving their sports program, or raising their academic standards. If you are knowledgeable about the financial aid of the school, you are in a position to negotiate and get a better deal than someone who is not.

Concerning a scholarship, it is likely that you never will get one. Even if, by chance, a contributor offers one, it is likely not going to be much. Now it is true that there are late bloomers. Some scholarship providers even recognize these old diamonds in the rough in need of gold or cold cash. With the merit and academic scholarship, you need to ensure that your child has a strong GPA, performs well on the standardized tests and is more than just a student but has many outside activities involving the community.

With a financial expert, it is possible to find scholarships for virtually any group under the sun. There are religious scholarships, racial and ethnic scholarships—you name it! It is a matter of spending hours finding it or placing your scholarship financial expert with the software and the skills to pull several needles out of a haystack.

When calculating the cost of college, you must keep in mind the following steps to apply to college:

- Ensure it fits with your major through career assessment tests, careful exploration of each campus so that they are not significant hopping, bar hopping, or settling for a college not of their choosing.
- Budget to determine how much you want to spend.
- Position yourself to get the price.
- Understand the percentages for financial need met as well as rates of grant aid.
- Explore financial strategies like maximum aid stratgies.

An excellent way to jumpstart the career-planning process is to receive career assessments. Additionally, it is essential to understand the dynamics of the college of their choice. While an understanding of the finances of attending college is vital, academics should be the primary focus. All the money in the world will never be a substitute for academic ability and accomplishment. Even if John "Bluto" Blutarsky's (John Belushi) parents have a lot of money, that should not be enough to get him accepted to college.

Understand the cost of your college from the perspective of admissions. Applying to about six to eight schools is essential because if we only apply to one, the financial aid officer says, "I'm the only game in town. They want to come to my school, and I have no competition. They'll pay what I ask." Applying makes a student seem desirable to an admission officer.

Keep in mind that there is an application fee, so if you apply to more than eight schools, the application costs could be high. Looking at the college admission process through the eyes of the admissions officer, you want to show that you have been offered rates that are less so that you have the bargaining power to lower the cost of the college of your choice. You may not even want to go to half of the schools you applied to, but the college of your choice does not want to lose an excellent student to another school so that you can use this knowledge as a bargaining tool. Ultimately, always know that you have many choices.

Realize that the exorbitant cost of college isn't absolute. By repositioning your assets, carefully selecting the right college, and negotiating with admission, the college of your choice may be within your reach. The next step in college planning is to choose the proper housing because where you live is a significant factor in college planning.

CHAPTER 14

College Admissions on the House

Housing is absolutely essential to human flourishing. Without stable shelter, it all falls apart.
Matthew Desmond.

While selecting the college of your dreams, keep in mind that where you live-on or off-campus will drastically determine the quality of your college life. Your house is your home base. It is the place where you will rest, regroup. Make sure you choose your housing wisely.

What parents and teachers and you need to understand about planning to get into the college of your choice is to recognize that the emphasis for preparation should be aimed toward retention, not merely getting accepted. Why? Many students do not know how to sustain themselves. According to Kevina Brown, Community Relations Specialist at San Jose State University, years ago, the emphasis was going to college since many chose trade jobs. Now the goal is to not just attend but complete college. For many students, especially young ones fresh out of high school, completing a college degree on time is extremely challenging. The reason being is that many students do not realize that there is a wealth of resources at their fingertips. A lot of students do not know that if they need help with tutoring, there is a tutoring center available (Brown). If they need help with writing, there is a Writing Center open. There are math labs where they can receive tutoring. Sometimes when they stumble, they just kind of stay there. According to Kevina Brown, "The typical 18-year-old brain does not say I'm struggling, I need help. If you take advantage of these resources, you can get over that hump. You are going to stumble. It's not going to be easy for you at times. However, it is helpful to know that there are resources available to help you when you stumble."

When Should I Apply for Student Housing?

Aside from learning about resources available for tutoring and counseling, students must secure their housing as early as possible. In sought-after colleges, in particular, a house fills up fast. By the time classes begin, it is already too late to find housing on campus or nearby the college of your choice unless you miraculously find someone willing to put you up for a reasonable price. Early preparation is the key. The other thing worth considering is that housing is one of the most expensive parts of a college education. For example, in San Jose, students spend 65% of college tuition costs at San Jose State University on housing. Prepare early. Kevina Brown said that she used to advise students to prepare for a residence as soon as they decide to apply on campus. She says that she would like for them to apply whether they want to go on campus or not. "If you think you are remotely going to apply, do it. If you change your mind later, you can always get your deposit back" (Brown). With high rental rates in the area right now, you are better off securing housing now instead of risking the possibility of being placed at the end of the waiting list. Once you are at the bottom, it is next to impossible to work your way back up.

Is It Better to Live on Campus?

According to Kevina Brown, there is a direct correlation between students who live on campus and getting better grades. She says, "If you immerse yourself in the campus community, you are more likely to know about resources even if it's just a friend in the next room or even if it is someone down the hall." Kevina mentions that she developed a passion for specializing in student housing because she recognized the benefit of living on campus. When she first enrolled in college, she did not want to get involved in any student activities. As a result, Kevina fell on her face. By her third semester, she felt that she was at the brink of getting disqualified. It took her one full year to get herself re-enrolled and readjusted to the routines of college life and studying.

How Do You Keep Costs Down?

Kevina Brown suggests students apply to the halls that don't cost as much. Years ago, older homes contained comfortable and practical, community-designed amenities. New buildings, however, are designed as a suite-style or pod-style, which is not conducive to building a community like the older ones. The old buildings are brick Galley Style. There's a bunch of doors open. With the new buildings, you have to go through the front door and then through another door, which keeps students a little isolated. Students will have a better experience, generally in older buildings. Generally speaking, older buildings cost less than new ones.

How Do You Address the "No Means No Law?"

The "No means No" law is covered during orientation when considering a college, and it is essential that parents and students look at the policies about how the school addresses domestic violence. San Jose State has an escort service that shuttles students to and from campus, so when considering a college, make sure that there are escort services available.

What Should Be on a Checklist for Admission?

Check-in with admissions to make sure that you are in good standing. Gather all of your documents. When it comes to housing, you need to make sure that all of your admission paperwork is turned in on time, preferably early. The top three items to prepare are admissions, transcripts, and financial aid. It is essential to fill out a FASFA (Free Application for Federal Student Aid). You also need to know about payment due dates, which are very crucial because if you miss a payment, your classes will get canceled. You will be out, and someone else will take your place. Look into the health and wellness centers on campus. Before enrolling, students need to know that there must be a balance between school and life. There is no way you're going to survive without a wellness outlet. Connected with the wellness center is a mental health and counseling department that will ask you questions about your state of mind, your grades, and your goals in completing college.

What is the Price of Student Housing?

Since housing costs vary significantly from state to state and neighborhoods, it is impossible to assign a dollar amount. What one person considers affordable may be out of financial range to another. Victor Culatta is a seasoned real estate professional who designed many student housing facilities throughout California. He is an experienced professional with design, financing construction, and property management for more than 25 years. He says that the cost of education is on a sliding scale. The tuition in California is approximately $598 per month (Culatta). Realize that if you are paying for someone's tuition, you are not paying for their education–the tuition pays for the classroom. It's the fees that are killing people. Education is a small cost of going to school. Scholarships and financial aid typically offset the expenses. Awards can include everything from athletics, political affiliation, and club affiliation. Millions of dollars go unclaimed every year.

The Dorm is the Norm

Dorms are a standard and fantastic housing option. You will be close to everything you need and have instant access to the internet, activities, and fellow students who share your concerns. Best of all, there is generally an advisor to help with housing arrangements and services on and off-campus. While meeting the demands and deadlines of classes, you do not want to worry about commuting. With dorms, your housing needs are right at your fingertips.

Location

In the world of real estate, there are three things you should always keep in mind: location, location, location. Where you live, and the distance of where you live, will determine your quality of life on campus. Ask yourself, how big is my college campus? How far will I need to walk from my dorm to my classes? Will I need a car? If so, how easy is parking? Is there plenty of free and open space? Are there designated parking garages? If so, how much are they?

Demographics

Do I thrive in a large communal setting, or would I fair better in a small dorm atmosphere with just a few students? Will most of my roommates be my age, or will I be surrounded by students who are sophomores, juniors, and seniors?

New Versus Old

Please do not be lured into the belief that a brand new, state-of-the-art dorm is the best choice for you. Is the pricing right? Are there activities and support services? Do you connect well with advisors and fellow roomies?

Bathrooms

Will you share a shared bathroom, or will you have your private bathroom? Pick a dorm with bathrooms that match your needs.

Amenities

One advantage of selecting dorms with newer facilities is that they generally have state-of-the-art appliances and features such as lots of closet space, wall to wall carpeting, and excellent lighting, plenty of space to study and heating and air conditioning that work. How necessary are these amenities for you?

Housing with Fraternities and Sororities

If speaking the language of sororities and fraternities are

not Greek to you, you might want to look into them as a possible means of housing. If sacrificing a little money and committing yourself to leadership roles does not scare you, go Greek! Sororities and fraternities can be great organizations to develop close bonds with fellow roomies while developing skills that could lead to new avenues of college study, scholarships, internships, and even jobs down the road.

On-Campus Apartments

While apartments on campus may not be located right on campus, they are a viable housing alternative for students who are independent, function well on their own, and need privacy. Typically, the costs of housing are part of the financing, so you will not need to pay outright for your lodging. Also, if economics dictates that you need roommates to offset the housing costs, you will need to screen carefully for others to share the costs with you. Make sure that the people you select share your standards of quietness, cleanliness, and timeliness in paying their portion of the rent. Think of your potential roommate, almost like a marriage partner. Remember, you will share a dwelling for some time in good times and bad, in sickness and health until death or graduation will you part. Make sure that your roomy is a match made in heaven.

Off-Campus Housing

If you determine that you would rather live away from

campus, you will have the privilege of searching on or offline for your own private space. The joy of occupying your own space and the responsibility to pay monthly rent and utility costs is your responsibility. You might need to find a roommate to help offset the costs. If that is the case, consider the following suggestions:

Clarify What You Are Seeking in a Housemate

If you are environmentally conscious and recycle paper and compost, make sure that the person you choose to reside with you also believes in recycling. Spell out your value system, ethical boundaries, standards of cleanliness, and neatness.

Arrange a Face-to-Face Meeting

Before you agree to share your living space with a perfect stranger, set up a meeting at a neutral place like a coffee shop or restaurant to meet with a prospective roommate to discuss your expectations and voice any concerns or objections. Sharing a meal is a great way to get to know someone's values, ethics, and integrity. Trust your instincts. Pay close attention. Does that person show up on time? Is he or she considerate, generous, and thoughtful? Remember that how your potential housemate shows up at the meeting is how that person will behave every day. Can you live with that?

How to Ask questions

Ask questions about their work, goals, ambitions, background, and values. Ask them what they believe about paying bills, sharing the same living space, and how they deal with conflict and problem-solving. Suppose there is an unexpected repair bill for the house or an unusually high utility bill, how would they address it? Ask how they would feel about sharing food? Is food communal, or should everyone keep their food labeled? Pay close attention not only to the responses but also to the tone and demeanor. Any sign of detachment, hostility or defensiveness is a red flag. Trust your instincts. Your home is your castle, your comfort spot, your retreat from the challenges of daily living. You do not need to add the additional stress of a difficult housemate. Safeguard your emotional wellbeing. Your soul is not open to anyone in the house.

Coaches

Although I address scholarships in chapter 12, I cannot emphasize the importance of paying close attention to securing as much free money as possible when it comes to housing. Victor Culatta emphasizes that securing a coach for scholarships, writing winning essays, and obtaining affordable housing is a must to get the most of your education. The best and the brightest have coaches. Athletes have coaches. Successful real estate agents have coaches. Successful writers have coaches. Housing advisors can be especially helpful to students. With a real estate background, they can conduct a market analysis to determine the average cost of housing in a given area to obtain the housing that costs the least. There are various tools online to get this information. Students and their families need to evaluate the following when exploring housing options:

Questions Students Must Ask in Search for Scholarships for Housing

The first step in obtaining different, according to Victor Culatta, is to realize who you are by putting together a résumé. As you do this, ask yourself:

- Who am I?
- What have I done?
- Who did I volunteer for as a high school student in my church or my community?
- What is my identity? Am I African American and a member of the NAACP? Am I a Native American?

The Cost of Student Housing to Tuition

The cost of housing will vary depending on where you intend to go to college. Victor Culatta says, "You can't generalize housing costs with college because it is like comparing apples and oranges. Housing costs in the Midwest are lower than those in the Bay Area. Stanford charges a flat rate, so you will pay the same, whether you live in the worst or the best housing." To uncover these facts, a student needs to do lots of preparation to find the right housing at the correct cost in the right location.

How Many Students Look at where they live?

High school students of privilege do exceptionally

well. Victor Culatta says, "Housing advisors love to speak with students because education is important to us all." Housing advisors must meet with students at their high school or colleges. Student advisors can talk with parents as well as with students. UC Berkeley has Cal Day. Every college and university has an open house day. As Victor Culatta states, "The hardest word that a parent says to their kid the day they leave is 'goodbye.'" The goodbye is not the typical teary-eyed kind. It is often arguments. Therefore, the college, the parents, and the students must all be on the same page. There needs to be open communication about when tuition and housing fees are due. Again, it all comes down to planning early. It is never too late to start the conversation. Start the admissions essay when you're in elementary school. With a blank piece of paper, you now have a tool to prompt you to action.

How Do the Needy Find Resources for College Housing?

While many believe that housing and tuition costs are through the roof, everybody knows somebody. There are less than six degrees of separation. Even the poorest of poor people know someone with a good job. The preacher at church probably went to school. They probably know someone who works at a college or university. Also, people have a misnomer about college professors. Victor Culatta emphasizes, "Professor's aren't the folks who make a lot of money. They live in ordinary neighborhoods.

Only the noble prize professors who live in the Berkeley Hills and Cupertino are affluent. The majority of professors live in ordinary neighborhoods with students because that is what they can afford."

Remember that everyone is approachable. Some people, however, are afraid of asking those with money. Some are afraid to speak with those who are sick. Some people only see it through their lenses. People need to ask when they need something. If you don't ask, you are not going to get it. The worst thing that will happen if you ask for something is not that someone is going to kill you; they'll simply say "no." They will either say, "No, I can't help you" or "No, I won't help you". Then you should ask, "Do you know someone who can?" Some people ask for a job, and that's the end. They never follow up. You must continue applying until you get one.

How Do Students Choose the Right Housing?

In some colleges, the college chooses the housing, and the student has little say about it. If they are privileged or not, that will depend on what they can afford and what they cannot. There are specific apartments or facilities, whereas a particular group of students has always lived.

Developing a great relationship will not only help you with obtaining housing; you will receive tremendous benefits in getting scholarships and unique accommodation. Since housing directors already have a connection with **EOPS (Extended**

Opportunity Programs and Services). EOP is a comprehensive program to promote the academic success of students with educational and economic disadvantages. Find out if there are housing staff members who are EOP trained.

Keep in mind that if you prepare early for housing, identify resources on and off-campus to help you personally and academically, and apply for scholarships, you will be in a better position to succeed and afford even the seemingly unaffordable colleges of your choice.

Housing is one of the most critical considerations in college planning. Where you live impacts your quality of life, your college costs, and peace of mind, apply for housing early, and consider your living needs. Once your residence is secured, staying focused is the next step to ensuring you succeed in the college of your choice.

CHAPTER 15

Ready, Aim, Focus!

Lack of direction, not lack of time, is the problem. We all have twenty-four hour days.
Zig Ziglar.

Throughout this book, I have emphasized that regardless of your economic, academic, or family background, you can significantly increase your chances of getting into the college of your choice by realizing that you have options. On the other hand, too many decisions are the same as no choice at all. While college is a great place to learn many skills, make lifelong friends, explore your vocational interests, and discover your mission in life, college is also a society of distractions.

In chapter 2, I address goal-setting to get into the college of your choice. I am revisiting this topic because it is so easy to get derailed from your college dreams and drift into the rabbit hole of distractions unless you maintain clear, focused goals throughout your college career.

For all of you leaving home for the first time and entering the exciting arena of higher education, college life seems like a dream come true. That taste of freedom from parental authority has finally arrived! You can come and go as you please, eat whatever you want from the endless chain of fast-food restaurants and vendors around campus. You can go to bed anytime you want, show up or not show up to classes and choose from a buffet of sports and recreational activities that could keep you busy for the next hundred years. Not to mention, there are lots of exciting and diverse students and personnel strutting around campus to capture your eyes and your heart.

Besides all of these tantalizing diversions, you will get exposure to many fields of study beyond your wildest imagination. Brilliant professors, career advisors, and fellow students will challenge your current level of thinking, your values, and your FOCUS. Be very careful! Or, like the movie trailer from David Cronenberg's 1986 remake of *The Fly*: "Be afraid. Be very afraid!" If you enter the enchanting world of college without the conviction to graduate or devise a plan of action successfully, you will plan to fail. The breezes of distraction will toss you around like a paper bag in a windstorm. While attempting to breeze through college, I learned how a lack of focus could keep you out of the college of your choice.

My amazing and spiritually stimulating professor, Tom Bruce, at Sacramento City College once said, "Experience is not always the best teacher because you get the test without the lesson." My first-time exposure to college almost proved disastrous because I spontaneously took classes without planning. I naively believed my teachers would tell me exactly everything I needed to do to plan my classes. I thought they would be like adoptive parents. I did not know the unwritten rule that students are expected to be mature adults, responsible for their success. What a concept!

Unfortunately, no one explained that I am responsible for my success in college and beyond. Fortunately, after a few years of soul-searching, I pulled my head out of the sand and ultimately graduated from UC Berkeley because I developed a plan of action, consulted with faculty, associated with the right groups, and focused on graduating with laser intensity. However, my focus did not occur in one day. I was not ready to jump instantly into the stream of the Ivy League crowd right off the bat. To obtain the clarity to perform at the university level, I took most of my general education classes at a community college.

Christian Catanio, a student at Santa Rosa Community College, shared how taking classes at a community college has helped him achieve more focus in every area of his college planning. At first, he took a stab at attending Sonoma State

University with the intent of majoring in Lacrosse and Business. Then, life got in the way, and he realized that he needed an atmosphere where he could freely explore his diversified interests in music, business, and sports to pick the vocation best suited for him. He says that some of his friends randomly picked a major believing that if they were dissatisfied with their chosen field of study, they could change majors like switching a light switch on and off. What happened is that they burned through priceless money, wasted time, and still do not know which major is best suited for them (Catanio).

In chapter 17, I talk about how a community college is an excellent resource for adults returning to school. However, community colleges are also great for any college-bound student to explore options. For some, it is not necessary to attend a university immediately after high school. Part of successful college planning is recognizing that an amount of uncertainty is not only inevitable but necessary, especially during the first two years. Community colleges and uncertainty go hand in hand. First of all, they are so much cheaper, geared toward working students and people from unconventional backgrounds who need support guidance and time to figure out what they want to study and how they want to apply their knowledge. Plus, the transfer rate from a community college to a university is much higher than that of high school directly to a university.

However, many parents and some potential students mistakenly feel that admission to a community college is admission to failure. They think that the coursework is inferior to an Ivy League college, and their opportunities to get into competitive schools and great jobs will be compromised. Not true! Potential students and naysayers of community colleges need to ask themselves whether price should be the sole consideration of an education. Is there prestige associated with training even if that training comes from a community college? Some teachers in every college are more qualified than others. Catanio says, "the giant gist for the thing, in the end, the preamble for success in college, is not the college, per se, but how much you put into it. All the teachers I have ever had who are good at their job are passionate. They are involved. They care about you and how they deliver their lessons. I never had a teacher who was any good tell me, 'Here's the test. Bye-bye.' Only those who are clear about their academic and life goals should apply to the more prestigious schools." Christian says. For the rest of us who do not have a clue about what to do, community colleges are an excellent way to gain clarity and focus.

Nevertheless, even though community colleges are an excellent avenue for those of us who lack clarity in a college major, it is imperative to develop focus and not allow the many distractions of college life to derail success. All the distractions of campus life, the most insidious and subtle one is the distraction of your own mind. In the wake of fear and uncertainty, your self-confidence can be challenged.

The best way to combat negative self-talk and the temptation of real and perceived distractions is to create a written plan and stick to it. When implementing a plan of action, Christian asks himself, "What is the task? What will I need to get it done? When I see everything I need to do and write it down on paper, I have the confidence to know what I need to do." Make an outline, tree, or a roadmap that can take you from point A to point B.

Ram Sharma, a Wayne Morse scholar at the University of Oregon in Eugene whom I have mentored for several years, says that he learned the value of making a plan to organize all of his classes and activities. While in high school, his challenges began when he attempted to take several advanced placement classes and participate in a history club. When he did not receive grades that he had expected, he experienced a meltdown in his confidence. Fortunately, a caring math teacher helped him organize all of his daily activities and then prioritize them according to deadlines. She helped him calendarize his homework; make a list of everything he needed to do, then organize his to-do list based on what project was due the earliest. For example, if he had a paper that is due on Sunday, and yet has lots of reading that must be done on Tuesday, he should complete the paper first, then do the reading.

Brian Tracy says that once you set a goal to complete a task, take action immediately. He says that the key to accomplishing anything is to decide how to get it done, maintain the discipline to see it through, and be determined to get it done. He says that the key to success is to develop the lifelong habit of planning your day (Tracy, ch 2). Additionally, you need to develop the habit of success. The habit of overcoming procrastination, setting priorities, and getting on with your most important tasks is something that you can learn and master with continuous practice every day. When you complete a task, you feel a surge of energy, a boost of self-esteem that will make you feel like a winner.

The syllabus for each of your classes is your best friend. Use it wisely; refer to it often. It is your roadmap to completing your classes. Ask lots of questions and study intensely to succeed. You should ask yourself how you are going to prep for your test, which will occur in about one month along with several quizzes. Find out which exams require the most time to study and which are time-sensitive. If you have a term paper that is due in two months, start working on it immediately. Find out how much time each day you need to learn about it, research it, and then write the paper. Put down the dates in your binder. Be prepared to adjust due dates and tasks according to unexpected demands and predictably unplanned events. Life happens. Pencil that in your planner.

In addition to goal setting and scheduling, career assessments are a great way and an essential way to determine your interests and possible major in college. However, the problem with many career tests, according to Christian, is that they do not necessarily measure what you should ultimately do with the rest of your life, but how you responded to a test question on a particular day. He says that when you are taking the test, you do not necessarily ask yourself if the items question things you want to do, but rather, do you do them? You may not currently organize critical activities in a list, but maybe you want to make lists for essential tasks. According to Christian, the most productive career placement tasks would ask open-ended questions that enable the test taker the opportunity to come up with unique answers and creative solutions to solve problems. Instead of yes-no questions, the applicant designs the solutions. For example, instead of asking you how you feel about building a house, a more revealing career question might be, "If you have a piece of paper, a pencil and were asked to draw a structure for shelter, how would it look? How big would it be? Who would live in it? Why?" Knowing your "why" to accomplish anything is always more telling when taking advantage of career assessments.

Internships are another great way to gain focus. Along with study, internships are an excellent way to get hands-on experience in a possible career path and the chance to work in many departments without feeling as obligated to a regular job.

Many jobs that students get after college are typically through their internships. There are several great places to look for internships. LinkedIn is one of them. You see, not only will you connect with a worldwide network of like-minded professionals, you get to reach out to everyone you know who can help you. Internship.com is an excellent website to find internships. Founded in 2010, it offers over 100,000 listings from more than 60,000 employers. The best time to start an internship is during your sophomore year so that you have enough time to adjust to college life and your course load. A great, familiar, yet easily overlooked resource is Google. Do not underestimate its power and effectiveness in getting internships. When I typed "internships, English majors in San Francisco," not only did I uncover a treasure trove of internship opportunities, I found a site called Look Sharp. This site not only offers a cornucopia of internships, but it also lists scholarships like the Course Hero Scholarship, which provides a $5,000 award for new winners each month.

    Finally, joining clubs is an excellent way to develop focus. Let's face it; we are social animals and need the mentorship, support, friendship, and collaboration of others to succeed at anything. If you are not sure about what you want to be when you grow up or what major you wish to pursue to make your college dreams come true, check out some of the clubs on campus. For more ideas about clubs and other useful tidbits on college, check out the app Pinterest (https://www.pinterest.com/explore/college-club/).

Christian says that the fascinating thing about clubs is that there are clubs for every major. There is an accounting club, business management club, and a psychology club. "They are great hubs to branch out to see what you would like." As a student, Christian feels that clubs are so vital that everyone should join them. He believes that they are as important as all the classes you will ever take in college.

Based on my own experience as a student, I wholeheartedly agree with Christian. During my first year at UC Berkeley, I initially felt lost and overwhelmed with campus life. Since I was a 32-year-old reentry student, I felt nameless and faceless among my 18-year-old peers. Then, I discovered the Reentry program, and my life changed forever. I connected with other older students, volunteered as a mentor, received priceless information about financial aid, and developed life long friends. Most importantly, I found my compass and chartered my purpose-driven strategies to graduate.

Ultimately, it is essential that you map out a plan for college, stick to it as much as possible and yet be willing to change it when necessary. Know your learning style and how you plan to maintain focus. For example, are you an auditory or a visual learner? Keep in mind that attention is like a quiver of arrows. Each arrow represents a different part of college that you focus on: academics, socializing, clubs, internships, housing, and basic survival. Some people are procrastinators and never remove an arrow from the quiver. Some are impulsive and shoot every arrow without aiming at their target. However, to succeed in college and life in general, you must set your sights on graduating and fulfilling your life's mission. Get ready, take aim, and focus!.

By setting goals, you will develop the clarity, confidence, and convictions to complete any task, even if you find yourself in horrendous places that seem to arrest your progress. In the next chapter, you will learn about mindset, strategies, and funding sources to unshackle you from beliefs that college is not possible if you were incarcerated.

CHAPTER 16

Arresting the Misconceptions of the Incarcerated

It's never too late to be what you could have been.
George Elliot.

When faced with the challenges from poor choices, unfortunate circumstances, a horrific childhood, a broken home, broken dreams, college takes a back seat, especially to the incarcerated since employers bar ex-offenders from employment. Remember, however, that no matter how hard you fell, there are resources to guide you back on your feet. In Sacramento, California, Strategies for Change (strategies4change.org) is an organization that assists former inmates. The main focus is providing not just stable employment, but also union jobs. The objective of Strategies for Change is to provide long-term employment and education for former inmates at Sacramento City College Campus so that they do not feel outcast or stigmatized. According to Robert Hale, Forensics Programs Manager at Strategies for Change, "It is very challenging for them to be in an environment where they do not feel like they belong" (Hale).

The first step to enrolling, adapting to, and ultimately graduating from college is to develop a feeling of comfort by just being on campus. According to Robert Hale, "One of the most significant challenges inmates face is their lack of computer knowledge, especially the Internet. They become so overwhelmed that they drop out. The solution to this problem is to sign them up for some basic computer classes and walk them through the process until they feel comfortable. Things that most of us take for granted, like setting up an email account is challenging. Someone who has been locked up for 20 years doesn't even know what email means, let alone signing up for one. Computers are slowly but surely becoming the mainstream, but inmates do not receive enough training and support to thrive in this ever-changing and virtually competitive culture" (Hale).

Robert Hale says that contrary to what television predicts, prisons right now are just starting to train prisoners to use computers. Anytime an inmate wants to better himself, there is a lot of stigmatism among other prisoners not to use computers, and that is why many inmates shy away from technology.

According to Robert Hale, "People in there are not promoting change and bettering oneself." Promoting computer literacy in prison is critical because everything we do requires computers like getting a driver's license and social security. Many employment agencies ask for an email address, but most inmates do not even know what that means.

One of the great resources to help inmates develop comfort around computers is the public library system. They need opportunities to practice with trial and error until they feel comfortable. The problem is that inmates do not realize that libraries have evolved. When they visited the library as a little kid, books were the only resources available. Today, libraries provide a host of multimedia services, computer training, books to loan, and a host of educational programs online at library branches that cater to the needs of adults and children. Services like Strategies for Change can help ex-prisoners navigate through the many resources offered at the public library to help them acclimate to the Information Age, which requires knowledge of computing, and internet services. A strategy for change is a pioneer in the probation system.

Lee Seale, Sacramento County Chief Probation Officer, has been instrumental in providing many jobs, education, and rehabilitative programs, such as helping ex-offenders prepare for the GED along with cognitive-behavioral treatment. According to Robert Hale, "Getting employed is not as important as getting a person employable. Before you get a person plugged into a school, you should prepare them to be a student."

One of the significant internal barriers that prisoners face with getting into college is that they feel unworthy. They grow up in neighborhoods where education is unimportant. They are so concerned with putting food on the table that college is not a priority. The first thing they consider, says Robert Hale, "I've got to get a job. I've got to get some money!" According to Dr. B.J. Davis, Founder of Strategies for Change, he shares the difficulty inmates face, given their limitations of prison life. "Your efforts will only be as effective as your resources will allow." If I am hungry...*really* hungry, I am motivated to eat, and I am at a lake with fish in the water. If I have access to a fishing pole and bait, I'm going to be much more effective at catching fish as long as I am willing to put in the work than someone wading out in the water, trying to catch fish with their hands. I can put the same amount of effort into both of those activities, but they will both have different outcomes. Inmates have been so conditioned to satisfy the immediate gratification that they cannot imagine preparing for college, which is a great approach (Davis). Robert Hale says, "For them to see that far down the road is really hard, especially when they come from an impoverished neighborhood where that is not the biggest priority. Their peers and family will tell them, 'Why are you doing that? You need to pay bills?'" The challenge is just getting them to stick with the delayed gratification when they are struggling with survival. B.J. Davis says, "One thing that prisoners must do is let go of the artificial, survival mentality of prison life and do a pre-release, talk with a counselor. When you get out, it will be hard. You will need to make some sacrifices. You will do without for a while, but if you are willing to make the changes, you will reach your goal."

Enroll at your local community college. Be willing to ask for help and receive help. Pre-release provides remedial education and counseling to help prisoners adjust to the outside world. Robert Hale recognizes that "unless they have the support of family, getting through school can be a long and tedious process for them. Getting the bare necessities like a roof over their heads is necessary. They grew up with the belief that the good kids went to school; the bad kids went to jail-this is not necessarily true. However, their perception creates reality."

The key to helping an inmate reform and get into college is to embrace them, welcome them, and not treat them as outcasts. Making bad choices does not define a human being. Doctor B.J. Davis says, "A model of poor choices of the past does not define one's future." Along with founding Strategies for Change, Dr. B.J. Davis is an adjunct professor at Alliant International University's California School of Professional Psychology. He is the author of the movie *What is Recovery?*

Along with his doctorate, he holds a dual BA in philosophy and a master's degree in psychology and counseling.

However, in 1999, he was paroled from prison for the second time for drug-related offenses. All total, he spent more than eight years in prison. Not knowing where he would fit in, he enrolled in a community college and discovered two professors who inspired him. Through his interactions with them, he learned that in one moment, he could create his miracle. Today, he speaks with authority, conviction, and passion to those caught up in the system that our past does not dictate our future. "Everyone makes mistakes," says Dr. Davis. "However, you can use your mistakes to course correct. You can push your re-set button. Your mistakes can be a reservoir of wisdom. It is about redemption. It takes commitment, patience, effort, and help."

"Most importantly, you should continuously keep in mind that the past does not define you but refines you." Still, many may wonder why they should spend time and money on educating the incarcerated. The reason is that we are already spending billions on locking people up. Spending dollars on those who want to reform, contribute, and share their gifts with the world, and pay taxes is the better use of resources.

The Law Office of Jeremy Gordon (www.gordondefense.com) provides scholarships for the incarcerated. Jeremy's law office offers scholarship opportunities for ex-offenders. Jeremy is an experienced federal defense lawyer who helps clients fight for their freedom. He was a former prosecutor who has become an advocate for the criminal justice system. He is offering a scholarship open to all federal prisoners. There are no exclusions for offenders, except that they must be incarcerated in federal prison and possess a GED certificate. One lucky person will receive free tuition and books covering one three-credit semester hour (or equivalent) college course from an ACCREDITED U.S. university or college. The scholarship will be awarded four times a year via a contest. As a prosecutor, Jeremy discovered his passion for assisting the incarcerated by going to teen court while in high school. At first, he wanted to be a prosecutor because he believes in fair play and justice. However, after working for the Department of Justice for three years he recognized that many prosecuted for nonviolent violent crimes served cruel and unusually long prison terms. As a result, Jeremy discovered that providing rehabilitative services is the best way he can assist those to find their way through the penal system. Jeremy states that it is essential that services are offered to ex-offenders in the real world so that they can make real changes for themselves and society.

    Brandon Sample, an attorney, author, and criminal justice reform activist, partners with Jeremy after earning his law degree in prison. He graduated from law school about three years ago. Education has dramatically impacted his life. He shares Jeremy's vision of providing educational opportunities for the incarcerated. He encourages the incarcerated to use their natural talents to contribute to society, instead of warehousing them, maintaining them and providing them mundane, typical jobs like working on cars, making license plates with the sole objective of merely keeping them occupied. The scholarship presently available is offered to federal prisoners. For these scholarship programs to be effective, society has to change its views about the incarcerated.

As long as the prisoners have at least an associate degree, they are eligible to participate in the scholarship. Federal money is not available to those in county jails but is available to those in the Federal system, and they provide ongoing support. The Prison Scholarship Fund (http://www.prisonscholars.org) provides support and mentorship programs for prisoners to offer secondary education for inmates. The program is funded by individuals and through corporations and foundational money. To apply for the scholarship, a prisoner fills out an application online. The application award takes approximately two weeks once the application is complete with no quota as long as there is enough money to fund the program. According to Dirk Van Velzen from Prison, Scholarship, the program has been very effective at providing education and employment for the incarcerated. Historically, 110 people qualified from the 191 scholarships.

Of the 110 of those who were eligible, 74 received their release; one committed a crime, and the other violated probation, so there was only a 2% recidivism rate as opposed to the national recidivism rate for most prisoners. There will be a research project with a Microsoft program to track the recidivism rate of the prisoners. This information will be used to primarily track those released after two years to determine the effectiveness of the scholarship program (Van Velzen). It is essential to realize that as a felon or ex-offender, there are several grants and loans available for several different reasons, especially for college admission. It is easy to believe that there are few options available to you, but this is not true. If your income is $10,000 a year or less, you may be eligible to receive grant money, which you do not need to pay back.

    Grants may be offered for felons by the state in which you live or by the federal government. Even some private institutions offer grants. For instance, the Department of Labor grants covers different things like housing and transportation. To get an exhaustive listing of the many types of government grants available, check out Grants.gov. In terms of education, you may qualify for Pell Grants. These are open to almost all felons. Even though drug-related offenses may bar you from receiving a grant, you can overcome this barrier by completing a drug and rehabilitation program and passing a random drug test. While aspiring students with a criminal background may have limited eligibility to receive federal aid, you can overcome most of those barriers one way or another.

    In addition to grants, there are scholarships for felons. As mentioned before, the Prison Scholarship fund is an excellent resource to uncover scholarship money. Generally speaking, scholarships are similar to grants. The main difference is where the source of the money Organizations or schools donate scholarships. You do not need to pay them back. It is essential to apply for as many scholarships as possible. For an exhaustive listing of available scholarships, visit scholarships.org. There are scholarships available for just about everything you can imagine. Whether you are a member of a religious group, a specific ethnicity, or a cancer survivor, there is a scholarship somewhere that is just right for you. The first step to finding one of these scholarships is to make a list of your attributes, your religious beliefs and background, hobbies, interests, and unique talents. If you are the first one in your family to go to college, there might be a scholarship just for you. While most think of scholarships as an award for those with a positive track record in school, there are some scholarships available for average students with a desire to succeed in the real world. With a trusted advisor, coach, or friend familiar with the college admission process, it is possible to find the right scholarship for you.

    Along with scholarships, check out the federal and state-specific re-entry services for ex-convicts. At Live Strong (www.livestrong.com), there are several resources to help you get back on your feet, despite the challenges of finding employment, housing, and social services. For instance, in 2009, the National Reentry Program was launched through funds by the Justice Department to help individuals in the penal system receive job placement services, transitional housing, and mentoring.

Additionally, there is the Faith-Based Programs and Community Initiative that became law in 2001. This program offers access to recovery programs for substance abuse treatment. Look into the Second Chance Reentry Program at (https://nationalreentryresourcecenter.org/projects/second-chance-act/). Since 2008, the Second Chance Reentry Program aims to reduce the recidivism rate of ex-offenders by offering services from the local communities and the federal government. There are funds available for mentorship, education, shelter, job training, and community colleges—the objective of the Second Chance Program is to provide transitional support and assimilation into the community. Money is set aside for family treatment, particularly for offenders with children.

The Prison University Project (http://prisonuniversityproject.org) is a non-profit organization that supports the college program at San Quentin Prison, an associate degree program, which is one of the only programs of any prison in the state of California. Volunteers who teach include graduate students, instructors, volunteers, and faculty members from many San Francisco Bay Area colleges and universities. Jody Lewen, Ph.D., and Executive Director state that the Prison University Project has such prominence that inmates gain status as being intellectuals. Several inmates will sit for hours at a time in courses that are highly informative, fun, and transferrable to a university.

To improve your chances to receive funds and services from grants, scholarships, and special programs, please keep the following in mind:

- Make sure that you understand the application process. If portions of the application do not make sense to you, speak with someone familiar with the application process to walk you through it.
- Organize and make ready all the identification papers and proof of residence.
- If you are applying for a grant, loan for college or a business loan, provide an outline of what you plan to do and why you need the financial support.
- Provide proof of your tax return.

Although the Internet may seem intimidating and difficult to navigate, it can be your best friend. You will discover many resources to assimilate into the world and get support from others who experience your unique challenges in obtaining a higher education and meeting basic living expenses. Check out (http://www.prisontalk.com/forums/links/O).

The bottom line is that it is possible to secure resources to obtain the higher education of your choice and resources to survive in this competitive world. Without a doubt, you will face challenges in finding services for housing, health, family integration, and programs to re-enter the work world and pursue higher education. However, there are resources available. As long as you have the right mindset, you will find the right people in your corner to help you with navigating the system. You will find programs to help you get into higher education. Dr. B.J. Davis says, "Success leads you to the next success. If the answer is no, what are you willing to do to make it better?"

Keep in mind that no matter how far you have fallen through the system of corrections, it's never too late to start over and obtain the college of your choice. Some people will walk you through all the steps to get the education, training, and support you need to turn your life around. In the next chapter, we will learn that you are never too old to discover your passion, your ideal career, and the college of your choice.

CHAPTER 17

Demystifying College Admission for Adults

Whatever you can do or dream, you can begin it. Boldness has genius, power, and magic in it. Begin it now.
Goethe. German poet, novelist.

Have you found yourself dreaming about college, but feel you are too old to go back to school? Do you wake up in the middle of the night with a burning desire to further your education, but years slipped through your fingertips as you dealt with many personal and economic challenges? Are you over 30? Do you feel awkward, over the hill, and impractical for daring to dream about wanting a higher education? You are not alone. Many working adults are either returning to school or beginning their college careers for the first time. The important thing is to take action right now. With boldness and belief, your college dreams may come true. However, it is understandable why you are concerned and skeptical about starting.

If you think that you are a non-traditional student for going back to school, know that adults over 25 are one of the fastest-growing populations of students. An NBC Business News article *"Back to School: Older Students on the Rise in College Classrooms"* states that in 2009, students 25 are one of the fastest-growing populations of students. At the University of Louisiana, "Students older than 25 make up 28 percent of the University of Louisiana system's 90,000-plus students. The average age of Louisiana Community College students is 28. In the University of Louisiana system, the average age is 23" (Guidry). In the United States, 16 million to 54 million may need to return to school by 2030 to increase their level of education or develop new professional skill in order to find work (Hannon), particularly in this new era of automation and artificial intelligence.

Why Go to College?

Even under the best of conditions, meeting these prohibitive costs is challenging at best. If you are an older student, you may have a family career, and other adult responsibilities that make the possibility of college seem impossible. So why add the prohibitive cost of college to your already taxed life? The reason is that despite the obstacles, there are many reasons to attend college.

More Money

If money is a barrier to your college dreams, consider that those with advanced degrees earn considerably more money. According to a national report by the State Higher Education Executive Officers Association, a high school degree will earn you an average of $30,000 per year. With a bachelor's degree, you could make about $50,000 per year. On average, those degreed with a master's, doctorate, or professional can expect to earn more than $70,000 per year (Loveless). Many business people told me that they felt going to college was a waste of time. They talk about the few shining stars who achieved wealth and fame without college. Tami McHugh is a real estate broker with an MRE from Realtor University with a BA in accounting and Spanish. She is the owner of Heritage Real Estate in Meridian, Idaho. She dispels the guru myth in her Master's thesis: "Education and Success in Real Estate." She says that a real estate agent can be successful by achieving the minimum required training. However, many of the top-performing professionals earned advanced degrees. Those with higher education are more focused, write better contracts, and appeal to clients in professional positions with advanced degrees. They are likely to apply the finesse and soft skills to provide the highest quality of service and consequently command the higher income in the real estate industry. Therefore, understand that with an advanced degree, you will likely develop the organizational and analytic skills that command more income.

Self-Esteem

Many want to return to school to because they want to improve their self-esteem. People may feel trapped in their job because there is often an income ceiling without a college degree. Higher education may be a window to gain more skills through courses, internships, and externships. Externships are similar to internships because they provide hands-on learning experience. However, they are shorter and provided by partnerships between employers and educational institutions. Self-esteem increases when you learn new skills and adapt them to courses and hands-on training. Since our social and economic structure provides few opportunities, a college education will give you a chance to expand your horizons.

Career Field of Passion

Kevin Caron, is a truck driver from Phoenix, Arizona who pursued his dream to become a sculptor by creating beautiful works of art in his spare time. Today, he has more than 50 private and public commissioned works that are on display around the United States. Think about what you love to do. A college education might be a way for you to develop your hobby into a full-time career.

If you are not sure about your passion when you begin, relax. You do not necessarily need to know what you want to do when entering college. Just realize that college is the common pathway to discovering new career opportunities that may be just right for you.

What you study in college may not translate precisely into your career of choice, or it might. The important thing is to realize that all the communication, conceptual, and analytic skills you learn will be invaluable in many positions. Plus, the organizational, self-discipline, and the satisfaction you will gain from starting and completing college will shape you into a well-rounded, more professional individual.

Concerns Facing Adult Learners

Will I Get the Most of My Education with a Demanding Job?

Succeeding in college while meeting the demands of a job is challenging. Still, if you can discover your "why" for attending college, you will find the right people and resources to help you in achieving your college dreams. My fiancée, Nikki, has always wanted to earn a master's degree in psychology for many years. Even though she worked two jobs and an internship that was more than 30 miles apart, she earned her master's degree at the University of San Francisco (USF). There are programs like USF that meet once per week for six hours. Negotiate with your employer about compensating you for your education or giving you time off.

What Should I study Since I am Already Making a Lot of Money?

You might be earning lots of money in your current job,

but are you paying dearly in health and self-esteem? Do you feel fulfilled in your ongoing work? Without giving up your job, take a few classes that interest you as you get familiar with the college environment. Would you enjoy taking a photography course?

When Will I Have time for my Family or Even myself?

Research the curriculum and select programs that match your interests and time constraints. There are several online programs. Choose physical campuses close by, if possible.

How Do I Deal with Guilt?

Be kind to yourself. Expect problems. Like I mentioned in chapter 4, expect the winters. They will come. But spring always follows winter. Learn from your winters! Have crucial conversations with your family about your college goals. Negotiate with them about your availability. Know that you are setting a positive example for your children by going back to school. You are encouraging them to set goals and pursue something significant.

Where Will I Find Mentors for Adult Students?

You never know where your next mentor will come from. In adult programs, the Dean could be a possible mentor. At USF, Dr. Pomerantz, the Dean for the extended program at USF, was Nikki's mentor. He wrote her letters of recommendation and told her that she could call any time of the day with questions (Myres).

How Do I Deal with Daycare During Classes?

Consider taking classes during the day while the children are at school. Find out if there are daycare facilities on your campus.

How Do I Deal with the Cost of Materials and Classes?

Although the cost of materials is high, there are creative ways of accessing textbooks. UC Berkeley has instituted a program where you can get a 3rd or 4th edition of a text for a fraction of the regular cost. At the campus library, you might get full access to study guides.

How Do I Prioritize Tasks?

Test the waters of your prospective school. Talk with professors about auditing a class to see if it will work for you.

What If I Feel Complacent About Going to College?

Refer to your vision and mission statement. Seek an academic advisor or even a life coach. Keep in mind that what you might think of as complacency is fear in disguise. It is painful to do the things we need when we don't want to because we have to. Keep in mind that what you might think of as complacency is fear in disguise.

Am I Too Old?

Some people will always try to discourage you from going back to school because they believe that once you reach a certain age, it is too late. If you feel too old to go back to school, consider my story. When I was 15 in 1977; I was staying at the Sea Haven Youth Hostel in Seattle to escape my abusive home. Fulfilling my dream of graduating from high school, going to college, and landing a professional job in the medical field seemed unlikely. I was a skinny, homeless youth. I had not attended school for more than a year. One day, I encountered a worn, weathered custodian at the hostel on her knees frantically scrubbing the stairwell of the hostel. When I told her that I was not in school, she glanced quizzically and said, "You better enroll in high school right away before it is too late. Once you reach a certain age, it will be too late! You'll end up like me working all day at a thankless job with no money and no future. I once had a chance. Now I have nothing! I am nothing."

At first, I felt depressed and discouraged by the custodian's forecast of my future. But in my heart, I believed that I could pursue my education regardless of my age. Though time passed, my dreams did not have an expiration date. However, it did not seem like I would ever finish school. Although I attended eight different high schools, I did not formally graduate from high school. Instead, I earned a GED. I took classes at a community college. Then, I graduated from UC Berkeley at 35 with a degree in English. Yes, I was over the hill—meaning I climbed the steep hill of academia and made it!

Though my road to higher education was curvy, uncertain, and unconventional, I eventually earned my degree. If I did it, so can you. Do not worry about age. Think about your goals, your dreams, and your mission in life. Richard Bach says, "Here is the test to find out whether your mission on earth is finished: if you're alive, it isn't." If you feel that you are not the right age to go to college, check out this link from Business Insider that proves you are never too old or too young to do anything unusual. (http://www.businessinsider.com/100-amazing-accomplishments-achieved-at-every-age-2014-3).

Am I Capable?

Another barrier many adults face is the false notion that they lack the aptitude to handle the rigors of college life because they are older adults. Brandi Madison is one of my clients. She is a 48-year-old who discovered that it is never too late to pursue one's academic dreams. Brandi is a hypnotherapist and an event planner for singles. However, Brandi said that she often felt inferior to those who earned advanced degrees. Obtaining a college degree has always been one of her lifetime goals. However, her stepfather told her that she is incapable of studying. Consequently, Brandi feared that she would never succeed in college. However, she discovered that with more education, it is possible to gain respect, especially the more educated she gets, the more respect she feels she can command, especially within her chosen field as an environmental scientist.

Strategies for Adult Learners

Consider Enrolling in a Community College

The community college might be your best friend, especially for adults, since the average age of a community college student is around 29 (www.ccsseorg/quiz.cfm). What's great about the community college is that it is perfect for students who feel uncertain about what they want to study or what career path they wish to explore. One reason is that the cost of attending a community college is cheap. Fees at four-year institutions can rise to thousands of dollars. At a minimal cost, you can complete your first two years of study at a moderate price. If you decide that you want to attend a university, a two-year college need not be your final destination spot. There are transfer agreements to virtually every major university. While attending classes at the community college, you can learn about what courses they require to transfer to a university of your choice. Then you can speak with a counselor and visit that university to gain more information.

It is a perfect transitional place, especially if you have struggled in high school or you are trying to balance work and raising a family while meeting the demands of college life.

Sandra Roddy Adams is a perfect example of one who worked, raised a family, and pursued her dreams. Even though she experienced much hardship and opposition from family, while raising two children, she earned her BA in anthropology and is a chiropractor in San Francisco.

Before You Hang Your Hat

In chapter 6, I mentioned the importance of thoroughly researching your college of choice. I am re-introducing this topic because adult students need to pay close attention to the logistics and physical atmosphere of their select college, particularly if they have special needs.

Every college campus has unique attributes. Jorge Escobar, Acting President at San Jose City College at San José City College (www.SJCC.edu), in California, is passionately committed to the safety and success of over 14,000 students at this community college. Jorge believes that students should first digitally explore their prospective colleges through websites and other online platforms and in printed forms. "If you have special needs, it is especially important to find out what accommodations are available, particularly if you are an athlete or someone with a different ability. Take into consideration your living situation and what kind of environment will meet your needs. In a perfect world, those resources should be easy to locate" (Escobar).

Equally important are safety and security. If you take classes at night, look for emergency phones and how well-lit your school is at night. Is there a sound security system? Does the campus receive positive reviews on social media? By planning, you minimize surprises for yourself and the college staff, trying to assist you. If you use a wheelchair and have classes on the second floor, there may be concerns. By recognizing your needs early on, you and the college of your choice can agree on a mutually beneficial plan.

To best prepare for college, keep in mind that everyone is an individual with unique goals and challenges. It all depends on the student and the needs of that student. Since there are over 5300 colleges and universities in the United States (Selingo), it is essential to know yourself, know the college of your choice, and how you will fit into a select college. While many students desire to apply to the top one percent schools, there may be many on the college menu that meet your needs. Age can be a factor. A high school graduate will have different needs than a retiree with a flexible schedule.

Enroll Part-Time During Your First Year

College can be an exciting, life-changing experience. You will learn skills, develop your writing and analytic abilities, make new friends, and build friendships and acquaintances who may connect you with new career opportunities and resources. The excitement and enthusiasm you may feel could be so intense that it is tempting to take a full load of classes and volunteer for every organization. Don't! Give yourself time to adjust to college life. Familiarize yourself with the layout of your campus. Determine how much time it will take you to walk to different departments. Keep in mind that more than 60 percent of all community college students attend part time. You can receive financial aid as long as you are taking a minimum of six units. Pace yourself.

As you gain more familiarity with the college environment and yourself concerning a college, you can enroll in more classes. The important thing is taking small, measurable steps toward achieving your college goals.

Screen Potential Instructors

Before taking any class at a community college and beyond, investigate your instructors. I cannot emphasize this enough. Know who will be teaching and grading you. Doing this one step can make the difference between earning an "A" or an "F." Though many instructors love their subject, teaching abilities and empathy toward students varies greatly.

Visit Rate My Professors (http://www.ratemyprofessors.com). This site will provide a snapshot description of how students have rated a professor based on grading, approachability, and the level of difficulty of the course.

Besides an online profile of professors, ask other students in person about their experiences with a professor. After meeting with students, visit the prospective professor during office hours for an informal interview. By visiting with professors, you will learn more about the professor. Since the quality of your college experience is in proportion to your relationship with your professors, you must screen them carefully. Think about testing a professor like buying a car. You would typically not buy the first automobile off the lot without knowing the price and accessories.

When you meet with the professor, make sure you visit during regular office hours unless you called in advance and made special arrangements. Then do the following:

1. **Keep the conversation brief.**

    Let the professor know that you only need 10 minutes of his or her time. He or she will appreciate your sensitivity to time. Most will be professionals who love to talk about themselves. Their willingness to fully engage you is a good indicator that they will be approachable in class and subsequent meetings. If the professor is curt, kindly excuse yourself from the conference and run like a deer in a forest fire.

2. **How easy is it to earn an A?**

    While grades are not the ultimate measure of a human being, they are critical to admission to a four-year school and for specific scholarships. If your goal is to earn straight A's throughout college, tell this to your prospective professor. Specifically, say, "I need to earn all A's in college. What exactly do I need to do to make that happen?" If the professor describes the steps to achieving academic excellence, that professor is an excellent candidate to take. However, if the professor says that he or she rarely gives A's or says that only Einstein can get straight A's, that is a professor you do not want to have.

3. **Grading.**

    Ask the professor: how do they grade? Are grades based on a straight percentage or a curve? What rate of the grading is based on reading and/or lectures? Can you receive extra credit?

4. **Testing.**

Are exams multiple-choice, short answers, or essays? Are they mostly open or closed book examinations? How do you accommodate students with special needs? In the unlikely event that I should miss class due to illness, personal emergencies, or particular work detail, how do I catch up? Do you give make-up exams? If so, what is the process?

5. **Instructor's expectations.**

How do you decide if a student is performing well? Do you recognize students who participate in class? What percentage of classroom participation determines one's grade?

Keep in mind that you must want to develop a close relationship with your professors. You want to visit with them after class and during their office hours as much as possible. Share particular insights that you have gained from lectures. Let your professor know about the unique challenges or concerns you encounter on and off-campus. Let the professor know that you intend to transfer to a four-year university. If you know which university you plan to move to, ask the professor if he or she is willing to write you a letter of recommendation and can refer you to colleagues at your select college. Do this early in advance and after you have developed a solid rapport with your professor. The influence of a professor can take you far in the academic world and beyond.

These are just some of many questions you can ask the prospective professor to determine if you are a match made in heaven. Bear in mind that you are ultimately responsible for your education. You are responsible for selecting the right professor at the right time for the right course. Only you know your living conditions, your working environment, your schedule, and style of learning. Some professors understand their diverse students.

You must join organizations on your campus. Check out organizations that support your interests, such as religious—and environmental sides. There are academic clubs that provide tutoring, mentorship, and academic advising. For adults, check out the reentry clubs at your university. Joining the Reentry program at UC Berkeley made all the difference to me.

When I began my college journey in the spring of 1994, I felt like a nameless, faceless person in a sea of other unknown, anonymous students; only I was much older. I felt alone, lost, and drained like a battery running on empty. I felt stressed trying to meet the seemingly impossible demands of college. Then I happened to stumble upon the reentry program at UC Berkeley, and my life changed forever. I made close friends with many exciting friends over 30. I received tips on financial aid and a work-study job with the Marin Institute due to my connections in financial assistance with strong alliances with the Reentry Department. When I look back on my college experience, the most important thing for me was not all the classes I took or the glossy diploma that hangs on my wall. It was the connections with my Reentry peers and fellow alumni at pubs, discussing all the ways we would change the world and affect public policy when we graduated. The Reentry Department was like a recharging station that fueled me with hope, optimism, resources, and, most importantly, the realization that college is more than just degrees, titles, and a gateway to a professional job. It is about forging lifelong connections and leaving a legacy of service. If you 25 years—or if you are older, join the reentry department at your university.

When applying to programs—and scholarships, some adult students feel unworthy. Know that you are worthy. You have applied to college to fulfill your purpose in life. The funding you receive from several different sources will enable you to concentrate on your goals and make the most of your talents. In so doing, you will be in a position to give back.

If you desire to go to college, do not let age, status, or income become a barrier. Many adults are returning to college for better careers, self-esteem, and personal growth. Keep in mind that adulthood is not a time to unwind and let your dreams slip down the rabbit hole of complacency and disillusionment. If college turns out to be the vehicle to direct you to a career you ave always wanted since childhood or an unrealized purpose the world so desperately needs, go for it! There are plenty of options for older students. If you are a special needs student, there are many resources in the next chapter to assist you.

CHAPTER 18

Special Needs and College Admission

You have brains in your head. You have feet in your shoes.
You can steer yourself in any direction you choose.
Dr. Seuss.

What Are Special Needs Students?

Students who were born with a syndrome, a terminal illness, a cognitive impairment, a learning disability, or psychiatric problems or panic attacks qualify as a student in need of special services. They may not be able to eat certain foods or participate in certain activities. They may exhibit social barriers, which not only interfere with the learning process but exclude them from fully functioning in society. In the United States, a clinical diagnosis is necessary to qualify as one with special needs.

Can Someone Be Falsely Mislabeled as a Special Needs Student?

In my approach to mentoring students, all of us are special needs students. We all have strengths and opportunities to take to the highest realms of our talents and purpose. We also have barriers that can sometimes frustrate us or delay us from achieving our goals in a timely matter. Frankly, I emphasize the gifts that propel students to academic success, rather than fret about conditions beyond their control. In a general sense, I do not believe in focusing on limitations. However, some of us have medical conditions or learning challenges that require treatment, additional support, and accommodations to make the most of our learning experience.

At the same time, some people receive false labeling because they behave erratically due to experiencing extreme trauma, abuse, neglect, or lack of advocacy to steer them in the right educational path. My school falsely labeled me as disabled. When I was in the second grade, I was placed in a particular education class because I was observed to be hyperactive and distracted due to severe neglect and abuse that I endured throughout my childhood. Consequently, I remained in special ed throughout my primary schooling regardless of what progress I made on my own because my school labeled me as uneducable. Back in the 70s, child protective services hardly existed. No outside agency investigated my unique family dynamics and the devastating effect they had on my self-esteem and educational development. Since I lived in a remote area, my abuse and neglect remained in secrecy.

Yet even though I received a false mislabeling, it does not negate the fact there is a great need to identify and support students with special needs. Here are some of the common ways someone is a special needs student:

Medical Issues
- Cancer
- Chronic conditions like asthma
- Congenital issues like obesity
- Diabetes and cerebral palsy
- Special Needs Accommodation

ADHD Symptoms
- Inattention
- Hyperactivity
- Impulsivity
- Poor social achievement
- Inability to access social situations
- Few friendships

Those with delayed skills since childhood may be eligible for special services or accommodations that provide individualized education programs in public schools that are free of charge to families. Keep in mind that the diagnosis of a disability does not automatically qualify one for an ***IEP (Individualized Educational Program)***. The IEP is a document developed for each public school child who needs special education. The IEP is reviewed often in a team. The disability must affect one's ability to do well in school.

A team of psychologists, occupational therapists, a special educator, vision and hearing specialist, and others are part of a team that will discuss, describe, and devise a plan in which specific skills or performance areas of the affected individual will receive the most attention. Professionals will work with instructors to ensure that the student gets the appropriate accommodation. Keep in mind that IEPs no longer apply once you graduate from high school. However, *Section 504* of the Rehabilitation Act of 1973 states that students receive protection against discrimination (Are There IEPs). When planning for the college of your choice, it is essential to know that even though colleges of today are more accommodating toward students with disabilities, only a small portion offer any assistance to a significant extent. Check out this list of 50 schools ranked as the most disability-friendly: https://www.collegechoice.net/50-best-disability-friendly-colleges-and-universities/

Public Versus Private School

Students with disabilities who are placed by their parents

in a private school may not receive the same services that they would get in a public school.

Preparing Special Needs Students for College

Again, even though there are no IEP services in college, they must provide accommodations under Section 504 of the *Rehabilitation Act of 1973*.

Standardized Testing Accommodations
1. Large print
2. Braille
3. Frequent breaks
4. Extended time on tests
5. Private room
6. Special lighting

Applying Concerns for Special needs

Along with the standard testing and application process of college admission have more significant challenges awaiting them. It is essential that they use even earlier than regular students to make sure that they receive all of their accommodations and that they are available when classes are in session. Challenges are awaiting them.

Questions to Ask Admissions:
- How many tutors will be available?
- Is my advisor trained to deal with students with learning disabilities?

- Is there any special technology or people who can help?

Strategies to Prepare for Admissions
- Prepare early
- Develop time-management strategies
- Experiment with technology
- Obtain recording pens for lectures
- Think outside the box be creative
- Prepare to address specific needs
- Acquire the *K&W Guide for Students with Learning Differences* by the Princeton Review

ADHD and College Admission

Students with ADHD may experience lower GPAs. Unfortunately, many do not receive testing until they reach college. However, the good news is that children with ADHD diagnosed in childhood may no longer meet the criteria for adult students. According to Doctor Eugene Rubin, an essential paper in the American Journal of Psychiatry reveals that there is strong evidence those evaluated with ADHD as a childhood may be absent in adulthood. A research team discovered that only 3 of the 61 kids diagnosed with ADHD still had symptoms sufficient for a diagnosis of ADHD when they were 38 years old. However, you must receive an evaluation from a medical professional to determine if you have ADHD. If you experience ADHD and decide that you do not want to disclose your disability, an assessment is still useful in determining the best path to take to achieve success in college. No two students with ADHD are the same. Some experience a combination of emotional, social, and other concerns that make transitioning to college especially challenging. These symptoms include:

- Procrastination or poor organization and time management skills
- Lack of self-esteem
- Difficulty keeping current assignments and reading
- Emotional and social problems as students need to make new friends with roommates and manage their stress level which is difficult for many
- Distractibility and difficulty focusing that leads to problems with math, reading comprehension, note-taking

Possible solutions to survive in college:

- Practice reasonable self-care
- Get plenty of rest
- Work with a coach
- Develop good time-management skills
- Seek medical care

Medication and ADHD

It is essential to monitor medicine for college students

with ADHD, immediately notify the campus medical department to learn about options. Students with ADHD must keep a note with them at all times. If there is not a health clinic on campus, a student should go to a local medical clinic and get a doctor's note. They must know what medicine they should take and how much in case of an emergency. Make sure that you store the medication in a safe place where it is less likely to be spilled or stolen.

Mentoring and Other Academic Support

Many colleges provide support for disabled, first-year students. There are orientations designed to connect you with departments, other students, and resources to make college life manageable. Having a coach to help you weather the college atmosphere is essential. Find out if there is a coach at your college or if you can obtain one from your local community. A consistent, caring professional can make the transition to college smoother. Waiting to see what will happen as opposed to seeking help will backfire on you.

Surviving on Campus with Special Needs

- Meet with professors regularly
- Get tutoring regularly
- Join study groups

Know Your Rights as a Special Needs Student

- Familiarize yourself with the ***FERPA (Family***

Educational Rights and Privacy Act)
- ➤ College students 17 years and older have an exclusive right to their records
- ➤ You must sign a release to allow parental access to your records

Why You Must Receive Accommodations

Accommodations will help you get all the support you need to process information from textbooks and classrooms.

How do you know you need Accommodations?

- You had them in high school
- You tried to manage on your own but experienced failure
- You need extra time on standardized tests
- You received a report from a clinician and received testing that indicated that you had been diagnosed with ADHD
- You have an IEP from High School

Types of Accommodations

- Extended time on tests such as the LSAT, MCAT, and the GRE
- Quiet area for study
- Note taker in class
- Priority in registration
- Late morning classes

- Class instructions are written out for you
- Reduced class load
- If you have been diagnosed with ADHD, you can have lectures read to you.

Know Your Legal Rights as a Special Needs College Student

- **IDEA (Individuals with Disabilities Education Act)**
  - Applies to students between the ages of 3 and 21
  - Colleges must provide services to facilitate movement from school to post-school activities
- **Assistive Technology Act**
  - Grants to help with the purchase of assistive technology such as voice amplifiers special software, computer hardware, and wheelchairs.

Questions to Consider for College Bound Special Needs Students

- Is the college in line with your academic and career goals?
- Is it welcoming of all students from a variety of diverse backgrounds?
- Does it have solid accommodations?

As a student with special needs, you should make sure that you get the medical evaluations, accommodations, and support services you need to perform your best throughout college. Recognizing your unique makeup as well as your talents is an important part of self-awareness that will help you throughout your college career and life. For those who are educators, families, social workers, and foster students, we will learn about the special makeup of foster students and resources to select a college of choice and succeed against all the odds.

CHAPTER 19

Fostering College Admissions Against the Wind

When everything seems to be going against you, remember that the airplane takes off against the wind, not with it.
Henry Ford.

Against the Odds

It was a deliciously sunny day on May 17, 1997. UC Berkeley's Greek Theater, I strolled across the stage and received my diploma. Later that afternoon, I met with friends to celebrate. During my precious few years at UC Berkeley, I had the privilege of receiving an outstanding education from one of the best public universities in the world. Every morning, I strolled by Sather Gate to attend classes taught by world-renowned professors. I made lifelong friends with many of my colleagues. I was the only student in my senior thesis class that earned an A for a speech I delivered about The Bronte Sisters. Today, I help many students succeed academically and personally. I help them get into the college of their dreams!

When I was 15, however, I ran away from home to escape an abusive home. I lived on the streets, temporary shelters, and with several different families. I could have listened to the counselors who told me that I would not make it because I was not street smart. However, I did not listen to them. I went to every public library branch throughout New York City and read everything in sight. Although I sometimes felt discouraged, I did not give up. Imagine, if I listened to the counselors, where would I be today? Where would my students be today if I had given up on myself many years ago? Imagine what you can accomplish if you dare to dream and do not give up! No matter how difficult your life might be, don't make the mistake of not fulfilling your dreams. There are resources and people to help you despite the challenges you may face.

A foster student is a youth placed into a group home, a ward, a private home, or other with state- certified caregivers, referred to as a "foster parent." (**Orphan, Foster Care, and Adopted Children** http://adoptedandfosterchildren.weebly.com/). Social service agencies or the government make preparations for the placement of a child. The institution, group home, or foster parent receives compensation for expenses. Although some mistakenly feel that it is a place where juvenile delinquents go, this is not the case. The arrangement of foster care is for parents who, for a variety of reasons, cannot care for their children.

Misconceptions about Foster Students

Many have heard about the negative aspects of the foster care system. Most of what people know is incorrect.

Tia Holiday, an instructor at Skyline Community College in San Bruno, is instrumental in fostering the Guardian Scholarship program, which provides financial resources and counseling for foster students. Recognizing that foster students have experienced severe abuse, neglect, and disruption of their home life and their education, she works closely with instructors to educate them about the unique challenges of foster students and how to instruct them best. Tia says many young people lived on the streets or have gone to a series of institutions, friends, or distant relatives who never adopted them.

Consequently, even though countless children lived under similar conditions as foster children, they do not qualify for all of the entitlements as foster kids who were wards of the court. Still, they might receive support from private individuals or colleges with their financial package, tailored to the needs of their unique student body. It is essential to research each school to determine which one offers the highest amount of resources and support. Before doing so, the first step is identifying the challenges of foster students and how professional liaisons can work together with school faculty to make college a smooth transition.

Challenges of foster students

I understand the difficulties of transitioning into adulthood without consistent role models. I appreciate the importance of self-esteem, self-efficacy, and social skills to thrive in employment as well as with friends and family members, for I was a foster child who lived in many institutions, homes of strangers. In places, one could hardly call home.

Multiple placements and multiple traumas such as abuse from caregivers, muggings on the street, neglect and a continuous loss of an array of relationships, produce additional problems like illnesses, lack of confidence, which translates into problematic relationships and feelings of insecurity. Every waking moment is the expectation that something terrible will go wrong. When youth "age out" of the child welfare system, they typically experience homelessness. Lacking the support of positive, caring role models, they are at a higher risk for mental illness, drug abuse, homelessness, or crime. They either fear going to jail or may end up there. According to Colleen Walski, Founder and CEO of the Scott Foundation, many foster kids think about death and dying. Plus, even though several organizations provide many services for foster kids, there are not enough people to guide them individually to acquire essential documents like birth certificates, driver's licenses and social security cards, necessary to complete applications. Since some adults broke trust, foster students rarely make it to college, let alone graduate.

For this reason, educators must take special care to understand how to work with foster students.

According to a New York Times writer, Michael Winerip, foster children are those who have been delinquent, abandoned, neglected, and abused, and that does not address the heartache, disappointment, and disillusionment connected with the unspeakable traumas many foster kids experience. Winerip mentions that even though most of the research on foster kids and homeless youth is bleak, a Chicago study tracked the lives of about 700 foster children in Illinois, Iowa, and Wisconsin. Those in foster care at 19 were less likely to have been arrested. On the other hand, the arrest rate is higher for those in other states where they had to fend for themselves. The Midwest study conducted by the Chapin Hall at the University of Chicago, those allowed to remain in foster care at 21 instead of 18, when most are aged-out, or mostly abandoned, would most likely pursue their postsecondary education (Winerip).

An Oasis Where Foster Children Thrive

Arizona is a special place because of its saguaro cactus, copper production, the Grand Canyon, majestic sunsets, magnificent colored deserts, and the Scott Foundation (www.scott-foundation.org) operated by Colleen Fedigan-Walski, Founder and CEO. After her son Scott tragically passed away,

Colleen demonstrated soulful resilience and purpose to rebuild hope by establishing an oasis for foster kids in the heart of Cave Creek. Inspired by his beautiful spirit and commitment to helping others, Colleen created the Scott Foundation to stay connected with her son and pay tribute to him by providing an atmosphere to help foster kids by impacting them through the transformative power of selfless service. Although Colleen has an extensive business background, she entered the non-profit world purely on emotional impulse to serve the greater good. Colleen believes that about foster youth, "When a flower doesn't bloom, you fix the environment in which it grows, not the flower."

Frustrated by the traditional business model, our severely challenged education youth between the ages of 14 to 17 for more than four years and even aged out, 18-year-olds needs family (Fedigan-Walski). Colleen turns Abraham Maslow's hierarchy of needs model on its heels. She emphasizes unconditional love and maximizing dreams and conscious living through experimental living. In Colleen's program, the Foundation's family role is to listen, facilitate action plans, and support the hopes to make a difference. What distinguishes The Scott Foundation from other foster care agencies is that it focuses on love, emotional well-being, and peaceful service, invested in their four-year future. Wards not only create a business plan, but they also develop a life legacy plan on how they want to show up in this life. If college instructors and administrators follow the lead of the

Scott Foundation, there is no reason why the enrollment and graduation rate for foster kids should not radically increase. On a basic level, there are a few things that can be done to make the transition to college smoother.

Essential Steps for Foster Students Applying to College

Sara Cohn and Rachel Kelly May from the National Center for Child Welfare Excellence claim that there are a few critical steps every foster youth must take to ensure a transition into college, a place to live, and a car.

Unfortunately, many foster youths do not get much support once they turn 18, so they do not possess official documents like their birth certificate and driver's license, nor are they aware of their rights. Therefore, a caseworker must walk them through these critical steps (Child Welfare).

Go to court hearings!

Foster youth have the right to attend court hearings and talk to the judge. Court hearings are an opportunity to let the judge know what they need and will seriously consider what they say. Every foster youth should actively participate in making decisions about their life. Also, they must get copies of all court reports.

Talk to an Attorney

Make sure you communicate with an attorney about needs and wishes. The attorney is supposed to represent the foster youth. If the attorney is unknown, it is the job of the caseworker to locate the attorney to reach out to the Office of the Foster Care Ombudsman for further assistance.

Get a CASA!

A ***CASA (Court Appointed Special Advocates)*** is a court-appointed special advocate. It is essential to have someone represent a foster youth in court to find out their needs and wants. Also, the foster youth may need help in getting records sealed after turning 18 if there is a delinquency record on file. An unsealed document will always remain open, making it difficult to get a job. The social worker and attorney can help with this process. To get more information on CASA, visit http://www.californiacasa.org.

Health

Emancipated foster youth during their 18th birthday may be eligible for Medi-Cal insurance until they turn 21, despite how much money they have or whether they are working. A caseworker needs to assist them in finding out what you need to do to get coverage. Foster youth over 12 have the right to see their case file and case plan. It is essential to advocate for them.

Money Available

Consider emancipation stipends. Some counties provide funds for 18-21-year-old emancipated foster youth. These funds can assist with housing, education, and living expenses. Ask your county's ***ILP (Independent Living Program)*** Coordinator. ILP provides money to youth who participate in the program as an incentive. Also, many programs have scholarships, grants, and funds for driver's training, computers, and recreational activities. College Financial Aid: Foster youth are considered "independent" students. Therefore, they are eligible for maximum state and federal grants. Financial aid not only pays for tuition costs but also helps pay for rent and living expenses at colleges and vocational schools.

Education

Welfare to Work: Former foster youth aged 18-25 are eligible for Welfare to Work funding for employment training, placement, and services. Contact the local county welfare department by phone to determine the closest Welfare to Work office in your area.

Get a Driver's License

It is possible to get a driver's license if a guardian or biological parent signs the Department of Motor Vehicles (DMV) form. DMV will also accept the signature for the foster parent, grandparent adult sibling, and an uncle. For insurance, a social worker or probation officer can sign the forms. For more information about services for foster youth, visit http://www.fosteryouthhelp.ca.gov/default.htm.

How Can Instructors Help?

Instructors need to understand most foster kids have suffered severe abuse, abandonment, and neglect of every kind. Sitting for more than eight hours per day in a classroom is difficult. Not to mention, many foster kids have been let down by adults who were supposed to protect them, love them, and guide them toward independence. Expecting them to put their trust in a teacher and enjoy our education system is a wild stretch of the imagination. Expect them to want to be anywhere else besides school, even though they will spend more time at school than with their foster parents. Even the aged-out 21-year-old foster student may display mischievous or rebellious behavior of a teenager, which is not uncommon. Work with them. Show patience and keep the following in mind:

1. Foster Youths May Feel Resistance to go to College

College instructors expect students to be independent, highly disciplined, organized, and high achievers. Yet, many foster students lack the support, the stability of a stable home, and the mentorship to meet the ideals of a college instructor. They spend most of their impressionable, young years worrying about losing their home. They always fear that they will wind up in the hands of an abusive or unsupportive caregiver. Or, they may wind up on the streets. They will need a lot of individual support to gain the focus and attention to listen to lectures and sit among fellow peers. They may need positive affirmations and directions to study groups, tutoring centers, and other supportive resources on campus. They may need information repeated. Though it may feel tempting to treat them "fairly" like everyone else, bear in mind that they are not like everyone else. However, with support, compassion, and understanding, they could graduate College and contribute significantly to society.

2. Learn About the Background of Foster Students

Teachers and counselors, as well as school counselors, often lack the necessary background knowledge for foster students enrolled in their classes. At Skyline Community College, Jacqueline De Angelo, a former foster ward and champion of the Guardian Scholarship Program, educates staff about the background and possible alarming behavior some foster students might display in the classroom and beyond. With more funding and programs advocating foster students, instructors are more aware of the concerns of foster youth than they were in the not-so-distant path. However, many schools are shy of these crucial programs, so it is up to professors and college staff to keep an eye out for foster students and how to best help them adjust to college life. Some of the background information cannot become public property. But intuition, concern, and awareness are public domain. Find out the names of caseworkers and spokespersons who have access to confidential information and seek their support. Knowledge is a power for instructors as well as for students.

3. **There will be issues of trust**

Since many foster students experienced neglect or abandonment by adults, getting them to place their faith in a college instructor is a challenge. Throughout their childhood, distinguishing between good authority and evil authority has been a significant issue for them. Even though they are starving for guidance and assurance from a trusting adult, it may take months for them to trust authority figures who want to help them. If they seem disinterested in lectures or completing coursework, do not take it personally. Their resistance is part of their journey, an ingredient of their growth. Work with them.

4. **Practice Academic Understanding**

As foster students are often behind academically, instructors need to be conscious of the fact that there will be gaps in learning due to instability on the home front. Plus, foster youth grapple with disabilities and traumas. Some may not have a home life geared to study. When assigning homework or exams, instructors need to keep in mind that their foster students came from the battlefront of the foster care system and may enter minefields at their current residence. Or there are sure to be gaps as a result of multiple displacements. Also, foster children struggle with many personal and emotional issues while in the foster home, and homework is often not the primary objective each evening. Instead, the psychological effects a student faces may take center stage at any time. Teachers need to assign homework with this in mind, being sensitive to their issues.

5. Be Flexible with Homework and Due Dates

Instructors can be priceless for foster students. They can make the difference between failure and success and graduating from college or dropping out. They may be that one rare authority figure who makes them believe in humanity. Be flexible with deadlines and due dates for tests, homework, and even class participation. Know that they already feel overbooked with anxieties and worries beyond the norm. They may have relatives in jail, or they may fear the wrath of the law themselves. Please consider this. If they have received a definite diagnosis for a disability, they may need a quiet room to study and take tests or extra tutoring. Offer extra help if need be.

6. You are a Role Model

Even though college is an environment of academic challenge and growth, many foster students have sadly never had a positive adult role model in their life. To add insult to injury, they never received encouragement from a caring, educated adult. Just because they are biological adults does not mean that they do not harbor pain from their tormented childhood. Therefore, instructors need to help foster students take small steps to achieve enormous progress in the college environment. Keep an eye on them. Check on them. Praise them for making progress. Offer to mentor them. Get to know them!

7. **Advocate for Foster Students**

Advocacy is a great way that teachers can assist foster students. Teachers and other school faculty must understand that children in foster care never experienced support, love, and guidance from adults.

Another school employee might be the first adult fighting for the child to have a better experience, championing for students. School faculty have the privilege of changing the lives of the foster student in a positive manner. More than anyone else, instructors can remind foster students about the importance of and the consequences of not getting one. Instructors can model, influence, and inspire students to follow in their footsteps. Knowing the psychology, the background, and the foster students is essential.

In "The Importance of matching instruction to a child's maturity level," Margaret Semrud-Clikeman, Ph.D. from the University of Minnesota Medical School, claims that even though the brain of children matures throughout life, the rate of maturity varies with each individual. Regular classes contain students with a variety of backgrounds and learning styles. Imagine the challenge a foster student may experience in a classroom since they have experienced severe disruptions in their education and family. Children who either grew up in disruptive homes or on the streets may not have developed social skills and a sense of fashion, or they may not be able to acquire it readily.

Independent Living

It is essential to participate in the Independent Living Program and take advantage of all the services provided by the Transitional Housing Placement Program. This program will provide valuable skills that will be necessary after emancipation. The Department of Social Services and the ombudsperson can help provide more information about this program. Service is essential to provide not only housing but also computers, means of earning money, finding jobs and housing, and scholarship opportunities for the school.

What Reaources Are Available for foster Students?

Though there is a great need for more services aimed at helping foster students, there are plenty of programs to assist them in achieving their academic goals. The problem is that once they are aged out, they receive little, if any, help in navigating through the murky waters of college admissions, obtaining documents to qualify for them and achieve necessary living skills. Consequently, they are not getting the help they deserve and need. They are like people who freeze in a blizzard three feet from their home because they lack guidance in finding their way through the front door. It is my mission and dream to provide a few resources for educators and concerned caregivers to help foster students get started. These sources are just a few to give scholarships, vouchers, coaching, and more:

Foster Care to Success: America's College Fund for Foster Youth

Foster Care to Success is a nationwide program that partners with other organizations, foundations, and individuals to provide scholarships to foster youth. Funded by organizations, individuals, and families, Foster Care to Success has been able to provide $1500 for books and supplies for one student each year, $2,500 to attend classes at a community college for one year and $5,000 for a university student. For more information, contact:
Foster Care to Success
23811 Chagrin Boulevard Suite 210
Cleveland, OH 44122
Phone: (571) 203-0270
www.fc2success.org

Fastweb

Fastweb is one of the most reliable websites that provides access to up to $3 billion in scholarship. Chapter 12 addresses awards in detail and numerous places that students of every background can receive free money for college, especially for foster students. However, I am bringing attention to Fastweb in this chapter because many do not realize that this fantastic website has plenty of scholarships for foster students. Whether you are a college freshman from a traditional background, a returning adult, or a foster student, you can find timely information on scholarships and schools. For foster kids, Fastweb could be a goldmine of unclaimed money. Many scholarship providers award aid for unique situations that include, but are not limited to, foster care recipients. Some of these scholarships are small. Others can be up to $6,000. For example, *The Foster Child Grant Program* awards approximately $6,000 for residents of Massachusetts. Another is the *John and Virginia McNair Endowed Scholarship* provided by the Hayward Community College. The *George Parker Memorial Scholarship*, provided by the University of California, San Diego, awards up to $2,000. The deadlines vary.

For students who are orphaned or parentless, there are several scholarships through several universities and colleges around the United States. Some of them overlap with foster students like the *Malcolm Stacey Memorial Scholarship*. Others are more specific to the parentless students such as the *James Howard Farris Scholarship*, provided by the Salem Community College. The award is $500 and the deadline varies. To find out more about scholarships on Fastweb for Foster students and others from unique backgrounds, create an account on Fastweb (www.fastweb.com) to find the scholarships, colleges, career advice, financial need, and other priceless services.

Chafee Grant Program

In 2003, the federal government created the Chafee

grant program which provides an annual $48 million in federal appropriation used to award scholarships of around $5,000. To qualify, a foster student must be a ward of the court, living in foster care for at least one day and between the ages of 16 and 18—those who have not reached their 22nd birthday as of July 1st qualify.

To apply, do the following:

- Submit the Free Application for Federal Student Aid (FAFSA)
- If you do not have a social security number, send the application, the name given to Assembly Bills 130 and 131, which allows some undocumented students to apply for and receive state-based financial aid.

The California Dream Act

(https://dream.csac.ca.gov) enables nonresidents and undocumented students to apply for and receive funded private scholarships through public universities in addition to state-administered financial aid, community college waivers, Cal Grants, and university grants.

Submit the California Chafee Grant Application online. If you are not able to send the application online, you can print a PDF version and mail it to the Department of Education.

Guardian Scholars

California has the most foster youth of any state, about

54,000, even more than New York, which has about 14,000. Created by U.C.L.A., the *Bruin Guardian Scholarship Program* is comprehensive to support former foster youth to obtain a community college, university, or trade school education. This innovative program boasts over an 80 percent success rate for foster youth who participate, as opposed to the annual rate of 8 percent for those who do not. The B.G.S. has numerous partners and connections to make study time at U.C.L.A. and other participating California-based schools as stress-free as possible. It provides the following benefits:

- Full Financial Aid Package–grants and scholarship packages cover tuition and living expenses.
- Housing–a priority for campus housing and availability of year-round housing, either on or off-campus.
- Academic Advisement–assistance with class selection & registration.
- Employment Services, Mentoring, and Career Counseling–job placement, shadowing and advising. Personal Guidance, Counseling, Tutoring–regular contact with a consistent counsel-or to develop and monitor an education plan.
- Supplemental Support Services–childcare, transportation help, book and supply vouchers, etc.

According to Jacqueline De Bernardo, a Guardian specialist at De Anza Community College in Cupertino, California, there is the *Guardian Scholars Program* that provides free grocery cards, gas cards, free scantrons, priority registration, and other resources for students. Also, *EOPS* is a program that offers support for anyone who comes from a disadvantaged background. There is no age cap. What this means is that even someone who is 30 or 40 years old could qualify for this program if that person were ever a ward in foster care. This program provides book vouchers, counseling, and help with registering for classes and a part-time counselor for Guardian Scholars who assists foster students with just about anything or puts them in touch with Jacqueline or anyone else who could help them. Though many schools have not publicly announced ongoing support for foster students, De Anza has wanted to implement such a program for several years.

Consequently, this community college offers help beyond federal programs because De Anza College knows that foster students need a little more pushing, a little more assistance than other students. They need to feel safe, supported, and appreciated. Although there has been much progress in jumpstarting programs, it is still a work-in-progress. The Guardian program does not have an age cap and awards meal vouchers. To qualify, a student must verify by an official letter. T*he Chafee Federal Program* however, requires a student must be under the age of

25. This governmental scholarship awards approximately $5,000 for every ten students. Applying can seem strenuous; therefore, students need help from social workers. Some colleges offer additional services beyond federal support (De Bernardo).

Collegescholarships.org

Collegescholarships.org provides a fantastic pool of scholarships and financial aid for a wide range of students, especially foster youth. There are several scholarships over $1,000. For instance, the *Dream Scholarship* offers a minimum of $500 and a maximum of $10,000 to applicants between the ages of 14 and 16 or former Chafee eligible youth who did not receive Chafee funds before 21. The deadline to apply is March 1st. There are several scholarships like this one. Check the eligibility requirements and know the deadlines when using.

John Burton Advocates

John Burton Advocates provide educational services across the state to help students achieve higher education. Finally, an organization that provides advocacy to ensure that all foster youth receive physical and mental health services to ensure their success.

THP-Plus

The THP-Plus (Transitional Housing Placement Plus) is a program that provides affordable housing and comprehensive support services for foster care and probation youth ages 18 to 24.

Technology and Educating Foster Students

Since only 25 percent of foster kids get a job while in high school, their chances of securing needed skills for a career are minuscule.

They are significantly reducing the chances of securing the skills needed for careers. *Teen Force* is a program that provides internships for foster kids to help them achieve success. Most employers who participate in this program would host foster care interns again. Interns learn Excel, accounting, website support, engineering support, quality assurance, and customer service. Learn more at Silicon Valley's Foster Care Summit or go to www.hackfostercare.org for information about how to help. There's a child in our community who needs you.

Foster Youth in Action

Founded by the California Youth Connection in 2008, Foster Youth in Action is an organization of young leaders working to ensure foster youths from different backgrounds receive fair representation. For more information, visit http://www.fosteryouthaction.org.

Together We Rise

Together We Rise is a non-profit organization committed to assisting young people who have been forgotten to regain their voice and society. The mission is to help young people navigate through the foster care system with ongoing support and collaboration of other organizations and community partners. For more information, visit www.togetherwerise.org.

CCAI

The Congressional Coalition on Adaptive Institute is a highly esteemed internship for those who spent time in the foster care system. Research is conducted to learn about policies that affect foster children across the country. For more information about CCAI, visit http://www.ccainstitute.org.

Foster Club

The objective of the Foster Club is to connect, educate, and inspire young people from the foster system to lead meaningful lives through a peer support group and people in the community. Foster Club educates foster youth about their rights and how to find the resources they need and deserve. For more information about Foster Club, visit https://www.fosterclub.com.

Every student who applies to college is unique with distinctive backgrounds, talents, and abilities to shine and contribute significantly to society. Though foster students have experienced many barriers and unspeakable traumas, they can make the world a better place if society makes a place for them. Flying against the wind, in the face of adversity, may be just the momentum that makes them soar academically, with the right guidance, the proper support, and encouragement from their community and their instructors. With artificial intelligence on the horizon in chapter 20, there will be even more excellent means to help foster students, and everyone else makes the most of their education. Stay tuned!

CHAPTER 20

Artificial Intelligence: The College of Tomorrow—Today

The Future is now.
Nam J. Paik.

We are living in amazing times because Artificial Intelligence (AI) is changing the way we study, apply for college, and select our career.

Do you feel amazed that your computer magically makes suggestions based on purchases you have made, movies you have watched, and places you have visited? Soon, AI will make suggestions about how to find funding sources for college, what classes to take, and how to shine as a college applicant. Understanding a few basics will enable you to make the most of your journey in college and this brave, new technological revolution.

What Is Artificial Intelligence?

Artificial Intelligence is a field of computing science that uses the information we usually associate with humans. It can mine through vast amounts of data to find patterns and intuitively find solutions through trial and error. Since the 1950s, AI's popularity has dipped and soared during the past six decades.

How Will Artificial Intelligence Affect College Application?

AI already automates CRM (Customer Relationship Management). It uses data at a rapid rate to analyze the history and preferences of customers to promote customer retention and sales. Artificial Intelligence may read essays, detect patterns, and decide what coursework and grading so that instructors can teach individual students instead of reading applications.

According to Jothi Periasami, an MIT professor and Chief Data Scientist at Experfy (Harvard Innovation Lab), AI will be used to meet the supply and demand of colleges in the future.

Not only that, but AI will also have the ability to gather all the collective intelligence in the world to uncover every possible solution in the world. A doctor treating diabetes, for instance, is only limited to his experience. AI will be able to draw from the experience of millions of physicians, treatment options, diet plans, and exercise routines that are specific to the individual (Periasami). Searches in Google are already getting more accurate each time we use them in the future.

With more than 17 years of data and analytics implementation and advising on AI, Jothi Perisami is the go-to person for an expert consultation, public policy processes, finance, and customer service. Jothi is an MIT professor. Jothi brings students a wealth of experience and knowledge. He works closely with senior leaders to standardize Big Data and its implementation.

Fortune 500 Company CIOs and CFOs have globally recognized him as the best subject matter resource (SMR) and delivery expert for extensive data.

How will AI impact the classroom?

According to Casey Newton in Can AI fix Education, Bill Gates is investing more than $240 million in a program called personalized learning in which private companies use software that will create lesson plans for individuals that will identify troubled areas (Newton).

The purpose of this program is to help students who are spending lots of money on community college courses but do not earn credit. As a result, they take many classes that do not receive them their degree. If they score low on remedial reading and math, they need to take courses that teach the entire subject. They do not tweak the results if a student is performing low in one section. If there was a personalized tool in place, a student could complete a module in one month or two instead of several months or even years as they are compelled to do right now.

AI plans to solve this problem by offering a personalized learning program designed for students. They will know many topics students who are falling behind in and receive personalized instruction from their teachers.

Although teachers will play a central role in the classroom, they will do less lecturing and work more on a one-to-one coaching basis. Education will be highly personalized, and educators will respond to unique personalities, ambitions, and living conditions.

Teachers will be able to create individual lesson plans. In the classroom, they will post announcements, assign work to students, and grade their assignments. Unlike remedial classes at Junior College, the individual platforms will be able to identify precisely which areas of study need the most significant level of concentration. Is it possible to complete a program within a month or two instead of several months? According to Tony Wan in "Real Questions about Artificial Intelligence in Education," there are AI systems that assist professors in delivering their lectures more effectively. For instance, IBM has partnered with Sesame Street in using universities as a testing ground for machine learning. At a hackathon at MIT, all the classrooms displayed cameras, with student consent, that spotlighted an instructor in delivering a lecture. If he did not look up to see whether his class was asleep, facial recognition programs depicted emotions such as boredom and instantly messaged them to the professor.

Additionally, a machine learning platform called TextGeonome is an infrastructure that employs deep, AI-based vocabulary tailored to students at their appropriate grade level. It will be able to determine what words are essential to learning at discrete stages and new words of the future.

AI will play a unique role in providing customized, relevant knowledge to learners as needed. For instance, Sebastien Turbot says in "Artificial Intelligence in Education: Don't Ignore It, Harness it" that intelligent machines will provide customized, relevant information to the classroom. For instance, he says that Content Technologies is developing personalized books to turn older books into related learning and study guides. As a result, students will use their time more efficiently.

Instead of presenting annoying facts, these individualized learning books promise to offer students critical, valuable skills that will encourage them to continue with their education yearly. Turbot even proposes that the new technology will nurture creativity beyond the limits of traditional educational practices confined to laboratories or summer holiday learning. Now, learning entails a whole new meaning (Turbot).

How Can AI Help with College Admission?

Administrators at Georgia State University contracted with a company called AdmitHub, an intelligent mobile messaging platform that helps colleges to navigate through the college enrollment process. It will handle repetitive tasks, collect data, and provide students with on-demand answers to primary admissions questions so that students receive personalized instruction from instructors.

An AI platform called Pounce developed by AdmitHub could support potential college students with their transition into college. Rather than provide general questions, Pounce targets specific tasks that individual students must complete ensuring admission. For example, students learn about the importance of financial aid. Those who did not complete the FAFSA would receive step-by-step instructions only on the FAFSA. They would not receive any instructions on other parts of financial assistance. Plus, they can receive answers to specific types of admission questions such as when does orientation begin? Where can I find parking on campus? What kind of work-study job can I take? Since college admission relies heavily on data and communication, Pounce is an AI platform that provides personalized support students need to weed through the jungle of the college admission process.

When Should Students Prepare for Artificial Intelligence?

Jothi Periasami says that "Elementary schools should introduce AI to children when they are in kindergarten. Those years are when children are developing their foundation of knowledge and will learn at their best."

AI and the Humanities?

Jothi Periasami says that before building a technological platform, you need to understand the underlying problem that the technology is trying to resolve. There will be a need for people with different talents and skillsets. There will always be a need for people who work well with others. For instance, there will be a need for someone with a business background. There will be a need to train others in the use and applications.

What Are AI Resources Available for Students to Apply to College?

Chat boxes such as Admit Hub facilitate services such as messaging, which is something that they do anyway through their smartphones. AI, avoids needless time searching through a maze of online portals and bureaucratic entanglements.

Along with chat boxes, AI technology can nudge students to the right resources by combining student behavior and interests with institutional behavior. Therefore, they can be directed to videos or an academic advisor, especially if they are thinking about dropping a class. AI can also employ modes to take advantage of all resources on and off-campus, such as transportation or access to distance-learning.

Students need to ask themselves what role they wish to play in applying AI to their lives. Will they outsource development and business activities? It would be essential to understand the framework of artificial intelligence both from the academic and from the technical side. There is a lot of free material on the Internet to learn the AI framework.

How can AI Help Students Prepare to Take Standardized Tests?

Test innovators founded in 2013 provide students with top tier test preparation that measures a student's performance with thousands of other students. It looks at variables such as time for questions and the question types. It can also point out places where courses need to improve. It will also interact with the way we work with information. It will pinpoint weak areas, suggest strategies to excel, and offer lesson plans specific to those areas of struggle.

AI will Impact the Way Students Research Information

Artificial Intelligence already impacts the way we gather information. Google adapts results to users based on location. Amazon makes recommendations based on previous purchases, and Siri adapts to your needs and commands geared toward your shopping preferences. I needed assistance in locating a computer store in a popular mall in my hometown. When I phoned, an AI offered me the choice of listening to whatever type of music I wanted during waiting time with pauses and humorous gestures like a real human being. Not only that, when I asked for exact directions to the store, it not only gave me the address, it pointed out landmarks and nearby stores. Imagine how this will impact how students apply for college, search for information, and look up facts as opposed to how students research information today.

AI Schools Find and Student Support

Right now, there are smart data systems that are already in place which assist with recruiting and helping students find the right information. Computerized systems mostly make every aspect of learning possible. However, AI-driven technology will ease the transition into college. AI may become a lot like Amazon or Netflix. There might be a system that will recommend the best schools and programs based on a student's interests.

How can College Students Prepare for the AI Future Today?

According to Daniel Pink mentioned earlier in chapter 5, the Information Age is transforming into the Age of Conception. Instead of traditional left-brained careers like engineering, accounting, and computer programming, right-brain occupations will rule. Design and storytelling will become crucial in the world of work. "Storytelling doesn't replace analytic thinking… it supplements it by enabling us to imagine new perspectives and new worlds (Pink, 108). What Daniel Pink means by design is that the careers of tomorrow will reward those careers with significance as well as usefulness. Hospitals are redesigning waiting rooms, and a young person designed prescription bottles with larger labels because she discovered that her grandparents were getting confused with the tags.

With AI on the horizon, these linear-thinking careers will require a whole new mindset. The college graduate of the future should explore careers in which they feel a passion for expressing their creativity and how they will contribute to humanity. Joseph Aoun, seventh president of northwestern university in Boston and author of *Robot-Proof Yourself: Higher Education in the Age of Artificial Intelligence* (MIT Press, 2017) says the solution to the AI dilemma is to empower young people with skills that only humans can do.

He calls this humanics "a discipline that teaches mastery of content as well as the development of particular skills. It helps people understand the components of the technical world while giving them the ability to utilize it, manipulate it, and ultimately transcend it" (Aoun, ch. 3). He recommends that all college-bound students should be schooled in three literacies: technical literacy, data literacy, and human literacy.

By integrating humanics with artificial intelligence, future college students will be technically prepared while developing mental elasticity to work well with others. Jothi Periasami says that Artificial Intelligence will never fully replace humans because people will need communities, family dynamics and will need to manage large companies and work well with other people.

According to Jothi Periasami, it is essential that parents and students embrace the possibilities of AI rather than see AI as the enemy. With the proper training, AI can help white-collar workers enhance human intelligence rather than feel diminished by this technology.

Humans Rule

According to Kai-Fu Lee, founder of capital firm Sinovation Ventures, AI will change the way we work and live. Still, it can never be a substitute for human interaction.

"Touching one's heart with your heart is something that machines, I believe, will never be good at all," he says. Careers that require service, collaboration, and empathy may be first-class employment. People will need real human effort more than ever in the Age of Artificial Intelligence. Nevertheless, it is essential to keep in mind that AI is the wave of the future. The AI Revolution will be larger than all of the revolutions of electricity, the internet, and mobile internet combined (Yan). Adapting to this massive change means that people will need to work closer together. They need to support one another on a grander scale, from the moment of college admission and throughout your career.

In the opinion of Jothi, students should learn everything they can about robotics. One way to prepare is to master Natural Language Processing (NLP). NLP is a field of computer science in which artificial intelligence deals with the interactions between natural human languages, computers, and the processing of computers to process natural language data instantaneously and productively. This technology is already in place. Siri on a smartphone is an example of this. It is now possible to speak into a wireless device and extract knowledge, find directions, and communicate with millions everywhere in the world in the blink of an eye.

NLP is already giving traditional jobs a facelift. For instance, according to Google Maps, there are approximately 50,000 fast-food chain restaurants in the United States and about 500,000 in the world. Of the several billion trips through fast-food drive-through restaurants, more than 50 to 70 percent of fast-food sales come from the courtesy of Natural Language Processing. It can eliminate hundreds of man-hour tasks by programming a robot to synthesize and extract precisely what a customer wants to order.

AI deals with financial institutions. For example, instead of waiting in long lines at a brick-and-mortar bank, it is possible from the comfort of home to push a few buttons on a mobile device and make withdrawals and deposits in the blink of an eye. Developing NLP skills will provide the promising student of today the opportunity for a world of work in the future, which is already here. A lawyer would typically build a case based on work experience and the scope of mental abilities. The lawyer of the future will be able to use artificial intelligence to extract all the legal matters across the globe and examine every conceivable possible case to come up with a solution.

Although many feel concerned about the impact of AI, this new wave of technology is already upon us. We use it to communicate, shop, bank, and prepare to enter the college of our dreams. Rather than avoiding it, learn from it. It can help you write better, search more efficiently, and study more effectively. It is part of the bold, new era of college admission that will advance rapidly, though it is upon us now. The college of the future is today (Yan). Adapting to this massive change means that people will need to work closer together. They need to support one another on a grander scale, from the moment of college admission and throughout your career.

CHAPTER 21

E-Learning and College Admission

Adaptability is being able to adjust to any situation at any given time.
John Wooden.

Even before the Coronavirus situation turned our lives upside down by forcing many schools to close and students to switch instantly from in-person classes to online platforms, distant learning and online education were inevitable. We are in a new century. The Industrial Age went out along with the last gas-lit streetlamp. While we live in an age of turbulence and uncertainty, we are in an unprecedented age in which we can access any type of knowledge and discover new information in a variety of contexts, locations and times. We can tailor our learning and college planning because of distant learning.

What Is Distant Learning?

Many confuse online learning with distant learning. However, they are not the same. Online learning refers to any cloud-based, web-based or internet program. Anyone can access online tools from any place at any time. It can include a stand-alone learning experience, or it can be an additional part of a blended learning experience. Distance learning, however, is different. It essentially consists of education transmitted through an electronic media that bridges instructors and students even when they are not together in a classroom. Typically, distance learning programs often require an on-site presence or face-time between students and an instructor.

Distant learning concerns geography while online or e-learning focuses on the mode or method of delivery.

Student Beware

Please exercise caution when selecting an online program. Just because you may need to take online classes does not mean you need to take the wrong online college program. Some of these virtual institutions of higher learning place profits over students and have been the subject of fraud, misrepresentation, and lawsuits. Don't get scammed. Be prepared. Make sure your online learning of choice meets the following criteria:

Is It Accredited?

Check to see that your prospective school contains the

proper accreditation, or stamp of approval to ensure it meets specific academic standards to ensure that you will qualify for graduate programs and receive proper preparation for your select career. For example, if you are considering an online program for psychology, make sure it is APA (American Psychological Association) approved.

The Department of Education's website provides a tool called College Navigator (https://ncesed.gov/collegenavigator/). This invaluable resource describes the accreditation of schools, graduation rates, as well as defaults on student loans.

Is There Support?

Whether you choose a brick and mortar campus or an online learning program, ensure that your select school provides you lots of support. Find out who will help you with registration, financial assistance, course selection, and troubleshooting of technology. In particular, ask about career preparation as well as degree achievement. If you experience any difficulty in getting the support you deserve, move on to the next online program.

Make Sure You are Technologically Compatible

Confirm the technical requirements connected with your online program. While technological advances have provided more options and greater flexibility, integrating this technology can be challenging. Find out from the administration or your college's website the required browsers and software.

Follow a Schedule

Do not be deceived by the seeming flexibility of an online program. Know the required reading, study time, paper, and research preparation.

Keep Focused

Recall the importance of goal setting. Envision graduating and obtaining the career of your dream. Normally, an in-person college provides built-in meetings and structure. With an online program, you must take full control of your educational experience. Begin your online classes with the end in mind. Chart your course. Plan every step.

Find a Consistent Working Space

In the brick and mortar colleges, students gravitate toward libraries, study halls, or their favorite coffee shop. Since you can be anywhere in the world while attending an online program, it may behoove you to find a consistent study or workspace. Consistency breeds security and predictability. If you program yourself to work in one specific location at a designated time, you are more likely to complete your studies with minimal difficulties.

Know About Online Tutoring Services

Find out where you can get support if you encounter any difficulty mastering the subject matter or any technical challenges.

Form a Study Group

Just because you are taking online classes alone does not mean you should be alone throughout your course of study. You can either meet with other students online or you can physically meet up with them at libraries, coffee shops, or a house. You only have one pair of eyes and one mind. Working with others allows you the opportunity to draw from the knowledge of others. Plus, you can develop friendships and emotional support. Take advantage of the power of connection. Reach out to others.

Ask Questions

Tony Robbins, the father of life coaching, once said that the quality of life depends on the quality of questions. With online programs, you must ask instructors whenever you feel stuck. Online courses are usually progressive. Week 2 builds on the information from week 1. Deadlines approach quickly. The best time to resolve your questions is the instant you get them.

No one can say with certainty which direction our college admission may go. But one thing is for sure: You as a student can choose to take control of your education. You can investigate the best online colleges, organize your time, get help when needed, and chart your studies so that you complete your program with style. As I have stated from the start, college begins and ends in the mind, even online.

FINAL WORD

Throughout *Demystifying Admission: Learn Key Strategies and Develop the Right Mindset to Get into the College of Your Choice*, my goal is to provide you with the resources and the mindset to make college happen. Regardless of your background, you can succeed in college and beyond. Developing your mission and vision of college admission, setting goals, planning, and taking action are the keys to unlocking the doors of the seemingly daunting process of college admission. Keep in mind that success in college and life is mostly a mindset. Know who you are, embrace the technological changes of college admission, and realize, regardless of setbacks or costs of college, you DO have a choice.

Good Luck,

Brian South

WORKS CITED

About Harvard, "Harvard at a Glance," *https://www.harvard.edu/about-harvard/harvard-glance.* Retrieved 24 February 2019.

Action, Annabel. "How to Set Goals (And Why You Should Write Them Down." Forbes. *www.google.com/amp/s/www.forbes.com/sites/annabelacton/2017/11/03/how-to-set-goals-and-why-you-should-do-it/amp.* 3 November 2017.

Auon, Joseph. Robot-Proof: Higher Education in the Age of Artificial Intelligence: Cambridge, MIT Press, 2017.

Bachus, Hermie. Personal Interview. 15 March 2016.

"Back to School: Older Students on the Rise in College Classrooms. NBC News. *https://www.nbcnews.com/business/business-news/back-school-older-students-rise-college-classrooms-n191246.* 13 August 2017. Retrieved on 25 February 2019.

Bayer, Justin. Personal Interview. 14 August 2017.

Brown, Kevina. Personal Interview. 15 June 2017.

Caron, Kevin. "Awakening As An Artist. *https://youtu.be/CX2b74iYUYQ*. 2 May 2018.

Cialdini, PhD, Robert B. The Psychology of Influence of Persuasion: Harper-Collins, 1984. Covey, Stephen. First Things First: Miami, Franklin-Covey, 2015.

Culatta, Victor. Personal Interview. 2 May 2017.

Davis, BJ. Personal Interview. 20 February 2016.

De Bernardo, Jacqueline. Personal Interview. 16 November 2017.

Dix, Willard Dix. "A Calendar is Your Best Tool in the College Process." Forbes. *https://www.forbes.com/sites/willarddix/2016/08/10/a-calendar-is-your-best-tool-in-the-college-process/#b3f21d34ddad*. 10 August 2016. Retrieved 1 February 2019.

Escobar, Jorge. Personal Interview. 6 June 2017.

Fedigan-Walski, Colleen. Personal Interview. 24 August 2017.

Givens, Mark. Jim Rohn. Zippy Zon Biz LLC, 2014.

Hansen, Adam. Outsmart Your Instincts: New York. Penguin, 2010.

Hartcollis, Anemona. "Getting Into Med School Without Hard Sciences." New York Times. 29 July 2010.

Hale, Robert. Personal Interview. 15 February 2016.

Hill, Napoleon. Think and Grow Rich: New York, Jeremy P. Tarcher/Penguin, 2003.

Hoffstadt, Brett. Personal Interview. 2 June 2017.

Holiday, Tia. Personal Interview. 12 November 2017.

Jones, Laurie Beth. The Path, Hatchette Books: New York, 1996.

Julyanto, Darlene. Email Correspondence. 16 October 2018.

Lovelace, Beckton. "Benefits of Earning a College Degree." Education Corner. *https://www.educationcorner.com/benefit-of-earning-a-college-degree.html*. Retrieved 25 February 2019.

Madison, Brandi. Personal Interview. 14 August 2017.

Martin, Emmie. "Here's how much more expensive it is for you to go to college than it was for your parents" Money. *https://www.cnbc.com/2017/11/29/how-much-college-tuition-has-increased-from-1988-to-2018.html*. 29 November 2017. Retrieved on 25 February 2019.

McHugh, Tami. "Education and Success in Real Estate" Journal of the Center for Real Estate Studies, Vol.2, No 2, pg 29. September 2014.

Myres, Nikki. Personal Interview. 25 October 2018.

National Center for Child Welfare Excellence. PDF *www.nccwe.org*. Retrieved on 24 February 2019.

Newton, Casey. "Can AI Fix Education." *www.theverge.com/2016/4/25/11492102/bill-gates-interview-education-software-artificial-intelligence*. 25 April 2016.

Onink, Troy. "College Costs Could Total As Much As $334,000 in Four Years." Forbes.

https://www.forbes.com/sites/troyonink/2015/01/31/college-could-cost-as-much-as-334000-total-in-four-years/#55b0e8fbc86a. 31 January 2015. Retrieved on February 25 2019.

Pease, Barbara and Allen. "The Definitive Book of Body Language." New York Times. *https://www.nytimes.com/2006/09/24/books/chapters/0924-1st-peas.html*. 24 September 2006.

Periasami, Jothi. Personal Interview. 12 September 2018.

Pink, Daniel. A Whole New Mind. Berkeley Publishing Group, 2006.

Powell, Farrin, "See the Average Costs of Attending College," US News, *https://www.harvard.edu/about-harvard/harvard-glance*. Retrieved 24 February 2019.

"Price of Attending an Undergraduate Institution," National Center for Education Statistics, *https://nces.ed.gov/programs/coe/indicator_cua.asp.* May 2018. Retrieved on February 24 2019.

Raghunathan, Raj, Ph.D. "How Negative is Your Mental Chatter?" Psychology Today, *https://www.google.com/amp/s/www.psychologytoday.com/us/blog/sapient-nature/201310/how-negative-is- your-mental-chatter%3famp*.

Robello, Steven. Personal Interview. 8 June 2017.

Roddy-Adams, Sandra. Personal Interview. 5 July 2017.

Selingo, Jeffrey J. "How Many Colleges and Universities Do We Really Need?" Washington Post.

https://www.washingtonpost.com/news/grade-point/wp/2015/07/20/how-many-colleges-and-universities-do-we-really-need/?noredirect=on&utm_term=.57223dbdf193. 20 July 2015. Retrieved on 25 February 2019.

Semrud-Clikeman, PhD, Margaret. "Research in Brain Function and Learning:

The importance of matching instruction to a child's maturity level." American Psychological Association.

https://www.apa.org/education/k12/brain-function. Retrieved 25 February 2019.

"Stanford Admission Requirements," CollegeSimply.

https://www.collegesimply.com/colleges/california/stanford-university/admission/. Retrieved 24 February 2019.

Smelich, Ed. Personal Interview. 14 February 2017.

Sophia, Yan. "Artificial intelligence will replace half of all jobs in the next decade, says widely followed technologist."

https://www.cnbc.com/2017/04/27/kai-fu-lee-robots-will-replace-half-of-all-jobs.html. 27 April 2017.

Tracy, Brian. Eat That Frog. Oakland, Barrett-Koeler Publishers, Inc., 2017. "Ultimate Guide to Choosing a Major, The" CollegeBoard.

https://blog.collegeboard.org/the-ultimate-guide-to-choosing-a-major. 24 August 2018. Retrieved on 24 February 2019.

Turbot, Sebastien. "Artificial Intelligence in Education: Don't Ignore It: Harness It."

https://www.forbes.com/sites/sebastienturbot/2017/08/22/artificial-intelligence-virtual-reality-education/#a1ad6c66c162. 22 August 2017. Retrieved 24 February 2019.

Van Velzen, Dirk. Personal Interview. 5 June 2016.

Winerip, Michael. Out of Foster Care, Into College, 30 October 2013.

https://www.nytimes.com/2013/11/03/education/edlife/extra-support-can-make-all-the-difference-for-foster-youth.html.

Wissner, Gross, Elizabeth. What Colleges Don't Tell You. Hudson Street Press, 2006.

TESTIMONIAL STORIES FROM STUDENTS AND PARTNERS

I am with pleasure, speaking on behalf of Mr. South, as he has selflessly guided me in so many ways within the last couple of years. I first met Brian through my father, introducing me to him because I so desperately needed guidance for an important final paper in

NATALIE ELAYAN
She received admission to Jefferson University's nursing program, the school of her dreams.

my composition class during my freshman year of college. He made it very clear to me in the most polite way possible that he would not be writing my paper, but I would write my thoughts or write what I can, and he would support me in how to correct it, whether grammatically or to strengthen the content. Being so far away, Mr. South did not hesitate to take the time out of his busy day to spend at least an hour with me on the phone to help me jot down notes for the rest of my paper and to help clear any writing blocks that I had. Any misinterpretation I had of stories that I was responsible for reading, Mr. South would kindly break the content down into the simplest form to assist me in understanding it better. He has significantly allowed me to grow in the areas

I was once weak, such as struggling to begin an essay. Now, two years later, I found myself in a position of needing advice for writing my college essay. Although this essay is more personal, the anxiety of thinking I might not be accepted kept me from being able to write anything at all. Brian was my mentor during this very difficult but important moment of my life. He suggested I speak from the heart, and so I did. I wrote my personal story on what made me even more eager to pursue a career in the medical field, including why I believe I am fit for the position in the nursing program at Thomas Jefferson University, my dream school.

Furthermore, two weeks after submitting my application, I received a letter stating that I had been chosen and given an opportunity to be interviewed for the program which is the standard process when considering accepting someone. The essay itself was so stressful and nerve-racking, let alone attempting to prepare for an interview! However, Mr. South assured me that my outgoing personality would not fail to demonstrate to my interviewers that I surely do qualify to be in their program. He spent time sending me more than 20 sample interview questions that interviewers would ask students. I practiced these questions with him over the phone. As it became almost an instinct for me to reply when hearing these questions, that's exactly what happened when attending the interview. Fortunately, I could not have been happier with the outcome of how the interview went. Mr. South could not have prepared me better for a time like this, and I couldn't be more thankful for all his help. I have been accepted to the BSN program at Thomas Jefferson University and could not have done it without Mr. South. I always recommend him to my friends and will continue doing so!

Natalie Elayan,

Jefferson University

Brian South's knowledge and expertise have been extremely valuable. He greatly helped my son on his path to admission to UC Davis. I highly recommend Mr. West for his excellent tutoring and educational services.

Mary Robb, M.A.

It is with great pleasure that I endorse Brian South as my educational consultant since February 2017. Brian has meticulously given me the encouragement and strength to guide me to follow my lifelong dreams to go to college and to pursue a degree in environmental science. As a mature student, I had doubt, fear, and anxiety about attending college. Brian gave me the support, guidance, and faith to believe in myself. My paralyzing fear and anxiety about going to college had begun to subside when I started working with Brian. With his expertise, I enrolled at De Anza College in the summer of 2017. His continued support and guidance helped me finish my first year of school with a solid 4.0 GPA.

BRANDI MADISON

She is a reentry student displaying De Anza Board of Trustees Scholarship only awarded to one student out of 18,000 students at De Anza College. She has a 4.0 GPA and received offers from elite colleges.

To continue to attend school full time, I needed to apply for scholarships. At first, I didn't believe I deserved to be awarded even one scholarship until I received the help of Brian, who believes in me. My experience with Brian helped me to realize the many hours I have selflessly served my community in the Bay Area while achieving unprecedented heights in academics and personal development. Filling out these scholarship applications helped me realize that I am as worthy as anyone else in my community in the Bay Area, while achieving unprecedented heights in academics and personal development.

Brian spent eight hours helping me complete many scholarship applications. As a result, I was awarded several scholarships, including the De Anza Board of Trustees Scholarship, which is only awarded to one student out of the entire study body of 18,000 at De Anza College. Being awarded these scholarships enabled me to continue to attend school full time without needing to work.

Brian has been instrumental in my success in school. As my educational consultant for more than a year, Brian has helped me pave the path of success in education. He has shared countless testimonials of other students who he has helped, which inspired me with faith to go forward.

As a result of the knowledge and personal development that I have gained working with Brian, I feel confident in continuing to excel academically, completing my higher education in great standing, and achieving my career objective in the field of environmental science.

I am honored to have Brian South as my educational consultant. I am eternally grateful that he is guiding me to achieve my dreams, which will allow me to give even more to my community and the world. I highly recommend Brian without hesitation.

Brandi Madison,

De Anza Student, Cupertino CA

While writing my college essays, I worked with Brian South of Choice Educational Consulting, to execute my application essays on time. Brian South was very professional and attentive to my needs. I really valued this because I needed to have my essays done in a matter of days. Before we started writing my essay, Brian called me to schedule a time that accommodated my schedule. I appreciated this because Brian was three hours ahead, yet he still adjusted his schedule to be able to accommodate to my time zone. My college essays were due in a short amount of time, and Brian was able to condense his three week program into three hours, so I would be able to finish before my deadline. Working on my college essays with Brian was an exceptional experience because he was able to give me crucial insight into how college admission officers look at and decipher an essay. During my experience, I was able to share my experiences and thoughts to put them into meaningful sentences. I enjoyed my time working with Brian because he was able to aid me in writing my essays with essential information and knowledge about it. Personally, I would recommend Brian South to any student working on or planning to write a college essay because of his amount of experience and his flexibility to work whenever you need advice in college essay writing.

Makoa Chinen,

Honolulu, HI

I have known Brian for about eight years as his supervisor and colleague in coaching the students in their academics and educational needs. I am always amazed by his passion, dedication, commitment, and wisdom for teaching and training the students for study skills development, knowledge enhancement, and improved performance in assessments and competitive tests. Brian is a wonderful human being and is highly dependable as a colleague. He is cooperative, punctual, patient, and extremely responsible.

I am a testimony for the improvement in the study skills of many middle school and high school students and their growth from a timid student to a highly confident student, or a low-performance student to a successful student. Brian has also been phenomenal in providing guidance, support, and direction to many high school students in deciding their career path in college. He has created a line of students who are critical thinkers and very independent and ready for college.

When I heard that he was planning to write a book, I was very excited because his ideas and genuine interest in uplifting the educational values and infusing the growth mindset will be very beneficial to students, parents, and teachers alike.

I wish him good luck in his dream to write this book and dedicate it to the students. I am quite sure this book will serve its purpose of educating not only students but also the parents and teachers.

Hari P. Shetty

M.S.B.A. (Info. Sys. & Business), B.E. (Engineering) STEM Researcher & Teacher

Director at EZ Tutoring & Educational Services

Brian South is a personal hero of mine. I want to give that full disclosure for the interest of anyone that would buy this book. After attending 3 years of Community College, I got into the school of my choice on my first try. I can't thank Brian enough for his invaluable assistance in this endeavor. I can think of no one more personally qualified than him for a helpful book like this. I sincerely hope that anyone reading it finds as much assistance from it as I did, from the author himself.

Erik Rob,

University of California Student

Brian Keith South

INDEX

A
accommodations 223
accommodations (special needs) 205, 217, 221, 222
   types of 221
ADHD (Attention Deficit Hyperactivity Disorder) 215, 222
admissions officers 45, 106, 113, 120
adult
   re-entry club 210
AI (artificial intelligence)
   classroom 251
   defined 250
   enrollment 253
   research 256

C
career 126
   assessment 146, 153, 176
   empathetic 73
cash value (life insurance) 147
Chafee (foster students) 241, 244
Coalition for Access Affordability 108
college
   cost of 17, 125, 144, 147, 153, 159. *See* also tuition
   distractions 170
   mission and vision of 112
   planning 41
   safety 205
college admission 25, 30, 39
   deadlines 99
   mindset 27
   planning 32
   self-esteem 198
college application 41, 103
   deadline 104
   early action 107
   early decision 99
College Board 79
college dreams 19, 29, 35, 54, 58, 60, 62, 170, 177, 199
   money barrier 197
college enrollment. *See* college admission
college funding professional 150

college goals 29, 47, 54, 59, 200
college major
  conceptual age 74
  planning 146
community college 104, 171, 172, 185, 191
Covey, Stephen 32, 34, 41

D
Davis, B.J., Dr 184
distance learning 264

E
EOPS (Extended Opportunity Programs and Services) 168, 244
essay 113, 114, 116, 118, 121
  questions 114
  steps to writing 122
  topic 118

F
Fastweb scholarships 131, 240
FERPA (Family Educational Rights and Privacy Act) 101, 221
financial aid 141, 233
  California Dream Act, The (foster students) 242
  discounts 126
  EFC (Expected Family Contribution) 143, 147
  eligibility based on class units 206
  FAFSA (Free Application for Federal Student Aid) 129
  FinAid 130
  merit-based 128
  Merit Scholarship 128
  need-based 128
  re-entry department 210
  work-study 149
Financial Aid
  Pell Grant 130
Foster Care to Success 240
foster students 226
  advocacy 238
  challenges 228
foster youth
  CASA (Court Appointed Special Advocates) 232
  Scott Foundation 229

G
Guardian Scholarship Program (foster students) 235, 243, 244

H
Hill, Napoleon 23, 31, 43, 60, 61
housing
  cost of 159
  dorm 160
  off-campus 162
  resources for 166

I
IDEA (Individuals with Disabilities Education Act) 222
IEP (Individualized Educational Program) 216. *See* also accommodations
ILP (Independent Living Program) 233
incarcerated
  Live Strong 190
  National Reentry Program 190
  Strategies for Change 181
internship
  defined 91
  self-esteem 198
internships 95, 113
  career 176
  CCAI (Congressional Coalition on Adative Institute) 247
  website for 177
interview
  faculty 80
  questions from interviewer 86, 88
  questions to ask interviewer 91
IUL (Index Universal Life). *See* cash value life insurance

J
Jones, Laurie Beth 19

L
lean startup 69
letters of recommendation 36, 41, 44, 95, 96, 100

M
major 65
mission statement 19, 20, 24, 60

N
NLP (Natural Language Processing) 259
No means No Law 158

P
Pink, Daniel 73, 257

Prision University Project 191
Prison Scholarship Fund 188. *See* also scholarships
procrastination 29, 32, 35, 41, 43, 50, 175, 219

R
Rohn, Jim 19

S
scholarship 133
  adult students 211
  course hero 177
  essay 136
  funds housing 164
  incarcerated 186
  Pell Grant 134, 189
  websites 138
Section 504 of the Rehabilitation Act of 1973 216
special needs 213

T
THP-Plus (Transitional Housing Placement Plus) 245
time management 39
  80/20 Rule 51
Together We Rise 246
tuition 144, 149, 152, 157, 159, 166, 233

U
UGMA (Uniform Gift to Minors Account)
  529 plan 142

V
vision statement 22
visit college 76
  admission office 108
  planning 77
  virtual tour 79
volunteer work 34, 44, 52

AUTHOR TESTIMONIALS

I have read many books on college, but this is by far the most comprehensive. Not only does it address the practical steps but also the invisible worries, doubts, and fears that plague most students when it comes to college. It takes you by the hand so you'll experience what to do to get in college, while at college, and afterward. If you are looking for a college admission book that has You in mind, this is it.

-Denver Vo, Hypnotherapist

Demystifying College Admission has been an uplifting and inspiring read, to say the least! There is absolutely no defined age to go to college as a young member of society, nor as an elder. I have returned to school countless times, taking various courses throughout my life and am going back again now at the age of 49 to take a business degree. Brian's book only adds fuel to the fire burning inside of me to learn and inspires me to be the best I can possibly be! In today's world of thousands of different schools available to us, it becomes an overwhelming task to even know where to begin.

This step-by-step guide relieves the pressures of decision making. It gives insights to make the seemingly overwhelming tasks of choosing what is best, into easily handled and achievable goals. Brian makes transforming your college dreams into reality and a doable event in your life. From the very first task of defining your very own mission statement to strategies for adult learners, this book holds the key to unlocking the very deepest of potentials in all who may have the joy of reading it. The depth and insights within will inspire all who are searching to better their lives regardless of obstacles on their path. The book is easy to follow and interesting to read, holding you captive from the very beginning. I was reading out passages to my daughter, who is struggling right now with the decision to return to school even though she feels she is not smart enough. This book gave her a new outlook on the whole process. I thank Brian for that as bringing hope to the struggling is not an easy task, but he managed to accomplish just that with the easy to understand wording. I highly recommend this book to all who have goals to achieve and wish to ease the task of college admissions.

-**Kathy Tuccaro, Author, of Dream Big!**

ABOUT THE AUTHOR

Brian South grew up on a farm in the picturesque region of Crescent City, CA. His father's abusive response to his mother's mental illness led Brian into foster care. His experience showed Brian how the system fails so many children, by neglect, by limiting access to education and by failing to provide guidance or mentorship in their lives. This cultivated in him a deep concern for youth and a love of education.

Brian lives his passion for instructing, empowering, and inspiring students of all ages and walks of life to reach their full potential. He tutors, coaches, and advocates for college readiness by specific subject instruction, mentoring students in college entrance essays, admission interviews, and providing invaluable assistance in sourcing college funding for students.

Brian is a lifelong learner, a dedicated student of self-development, and a champion of youth. He passionately shares his training and certification in education, coaching, financial literacy, neuroscience, and sales to help his students open the door to the college of their choice. Brian lives in Sacramento, CA, with his fiancée, Nikki Myres.

ABOUT THE PUBLISHERS

Cinnamon Tree Press is an imprint of Carnelian Moon Publishing, Inc., a hybrid publishing agency for heart-centered authors who are ready to birth their first or next book.

By working in partnership with you to provide a memorable and inspiring VIPXperience as you breathe life into your book, Carnelian Moon Publishing is with you every step of your journey from idea through to over 40,000 distribution outlets worldwide.

For discerning authors seeking a truly collaborative publishing experience, Carnelian Moon Publishing's team of professionals deliver support, guidance, service, and knowledge which encourages new, seasoned and serial authors the confidence to dedicate their time and attention to there craft, knowing the publishing details are well in hand.

With a defined Mission to provide guidance to 1000 best-selling authors in 5 years, infusing the world with empowerment, inspiration, leadership, passion, purpose, healing, and love, authors are finding the fresh approach Carnelian Moon Publishing along with their Imprints for Children's authors, male & female authors, and Metaphysical authors delivers, to be a perfect fit no matter where the author is on their journey.

Carnelian Moon Publishing takes away the overwhelm and challenges too long associated with publishing and inherently believes your authoring journey is meant to be a blissful one from your heart to readers worldwide. Their team of experts are ready to assist you in making your authoring experience an easeful, streamlined, organized, and personalized experience at every step. Whether you choose to self-publish or prefer to dedicate your focus to writing leaving the details to others, Carnelian Moon Publishing has the solution that is perfect for you and your vision, goals, and authoring success!

The founding corner stones Carnelian Moon Publishing adheres to ensures every step taken is in alignment with you the author and adheres to the Agency's core values:

- Authenticity & Truth
- Value & Reliability
- Community & Support
- Clarity & Focus

When the self-publishing author, children's author, personal development, or Spiritually-based author in you yearns to share your wisdom with the world, Carnelian Moon Publishing, Inc., is ready to welcome you to the Carnelian Moon family of exceptional authors.

Find out more about us at carnelianmoonpublishing.com

www.ingramcontent.com/pod-product-compliance
Lightning Source LLC
Chambersburg PA
CBHW071220080526
44587CB00013BA/1443